"Rich in reflections that will revive your mental health and transform the way you practice self-care, Rheeda Walker has masterfully crafted the ultimate guide to self-awareness, self-accountability, and self-healing."

—**Nakeia Homer**, well-being educator, and author of *I Hope This Helps* and *All the Right Pieces*

"This is a must-read resource for Black folks who face systematic racism and oppression every day. In *The Unapologetic Workbook for Black Mental Health*, Walker convincingly describes how racial oppression has shaped the mental health reality of Black people for generations by providing unique and complex insights while integrating psychological science and cultural values. She then brilliantly empowers the reader with skills to maximize psychological fortitude—fortitude needed in a society rife with racial discrimination."

—**Faye Belgrave, PhD**, professor of psychology, and associate dean for Equity and Community Partnerships at Virginia Commonwealth University; and coauthor of *Finding Her Voice*

"Chock-full of thought-provoking questions, brimming with concrete strategies and steps, *The Unapologetic Workbook for Black Mental Health* is a gift to every Black person who yearns to thrive emotionally and is ready to begin tackling the stuff that gets in the way—the stress of relationships, family and work, the impact of racism, and our sometimes-ineffective efforts to cope. This workbook guides us through it all. Wise and warm!"

—**Kumea Shorter-Gooden, PhD**, clinical psychologist; and coauthor of the award-winning book, *Shifting*

"*The Unapologetic Workbook for Black Mental Health* provides practical tools and useful prompts for Black people to engage in improving their mental well-being. Each chapter engages the reader with clear definitions of concepts, such as psychological fortitude and relatable examples of behaviors such as thinking traps. This workbook will provide Black people with a much-needed opportunity to pause, reflect, assess their mental wellness, and engage in the healing process."

—**Brandon J. Johnson, MHS, MCHES**, creator of the Black Mental Wellness Lounge

"*The Unapologetic Workbook for Black Mental Health* provides critically needed strategies for Black people to tap into their psychological fortitude and live the lives we wholeheartedly deserve. Rheeda Walker infuses her immense wisdom throughout this workbook to provide culturally grounded tools that center on the viewpoint that Black people have the strength to pursue therapeutic healing to help us further thrive. This workbook is refreshingly clear, affirming, and sheds new light on strengthening resilience and value-based living for Black people without, importantly, diminishing the pervasiveness of racism in our society."

—**Sierra Carter, PhD**, associate professor of clinical and community psychology at Georgia State University

"While there are numerous self-help workbooks to address mental health, most are only informed by traditional psychology which is limited in addressing the lived experiences of Black people. In *The Unapologetic Workbook for Black Mental Health*, Rheeda Walker masterfully combines empirically supported interventions with knowledge of Black psychology, history, and culture to provide a unique guide that empowers Black people to engage in culturally responsive self-care and stress management."

—**Kevin Cokley, PhD**, university diversity and social transformation professor at the University of Michigan, and editor of *Making Black Lives Matter*

THE UNAPOLOGETIC WORKBOOK FOR BLACK MENTAL HEALTH

A Step-by-Step Guide to Build Psychological Fortitude & Reclaim Wellness

RHEEDA WALKER, PhD

New Harbinger Publications, Inc.

Publisher's Note

This publication is designed to provide accurate and authoritative information in regard to the subject matter covered. It is sold with the understanding that the publisher is not engaged in rendering psychological, financial, legal, or other professional services. If expert assistance or counseling is needed, the services of a competent professional should be sought.

Distributed in Canada by Raincoast Books

NEW HARBINGER PUBLICATIONS is a registered trademark of New Harbinger Publications, Inc.

New Harbinger Publications, Inc.
5720 Shattuck Avenue
Oakland, CA 94609
www.newharbinger.com

The Anxiety Assessment on page 44 is reprinted with permission from Elsevier from "Preliminary Reliability and Validity of the Generalized Anxiety Disorder Questionnaire-IV: A Revised Self-Report Diagnostic Measure of Generalized Anxiety Disorder" (2002). By Newman, M. G., A. R. Zuellig, K. E. Kachin, M. J. Constantino, A. Przeworski, T. Erickson, T., & L. Cashman-McGrath. In Behavior Therapy 33(2): 215-233.

Cover design by Sara Christian

Interior design by Michele Waters-Kermes

Acquired by Jennye Garibaldi

Edited by Kristi Hein

Library of Congress Cataloging-in-Publication Data on file

Printed in the United States of America

23 22 21

10 9 8 7 6 5 4 3 2 1 First Printing

Contents

Foreword

It is literally exhausting to be Black in this country. Racism is pervasive and systemic. Anxiety, depression, and the suicide rate among Black Americans are at all-time highs. Self-care, when we do it, has only short-term effects.

In *The Unapologetic Workbook for Black Mental Health,* Dr. Rheeda Walker takes Black Americans on a journey of hope and healing, one tool at a time. At the end of the journey, the workbook will serve as a tool kit that uplifts us, sustains us, and brings us into the light.

And it all begins with psychological fortitude (PF).

Psychological fortitude is what sustained our ancestors, and it is what allows us in the present day to take care of work and school, manage our emotions, take care of our physical health, and tap into our life's purpose while navigating the threats to our success. By completing the exercises in this workbook, we learn the importance of and how to monitor our PF on a daily basis. More importantly, we develop "clutch" skills that allow us to replenish our PF when it is low.

This workbook shows us how to take values and beliefs that are at the core of our existence as Black people and draw upon them to become an unapologetic version of the person we are meant to be; for example:

- Embracing our spiritual self by reflecting and building on our religious practices in ways that increase our PF.

- Calling in Black, getting paid for doing so, and using the time to pursue the same amount of restorative pleasurable living as we are facing in challenges. This is known as *real* self-care and allows us to build our PF.

- Being specific—specific in asking for what we need, specific in what we believe, specific in increasing our PF.

Finally, Dr. Walker addresses the elephant in the room: Black folks and therapy. She lists *almost* every question *almost* every Black person has ever had about therapy starting with "Isn't therapy for white people?" Dr. Walker answers this and every other question openly, honestly, and unapologetically.

Though the exhaustion of being Black in the US is an undisputed truth, Dr. Rheeda Walker shows us in *The Unapologetic Workbook for Black Mental Health* that Black Americans do not have to live exhausted lives. This workbook empowers us with the strength to face and overcome the daily hassles and microaggressions and with the psychological fortitude to live the unapologetic life of our choosing. It is her gift to Black America.

—Angela Neal-Barnett, PhD
Kent State University, Kent, OH
Author, *Soothe Your Nerves: The Black Woman's Guide to Understanding and Overcoming Anxiety, Panic, and Fear*

INTRODUCTION

There Must Be More to Life Than "This"

Your intelligence is not enough to help you outrun your fatigue. And just because you're walking around and haven't had a mental breakdown, it doesn't mean that everything is OK.

You are descended from people who were brutalized for generations for profit and power. Those brave ancestors survived the best way they knew how. But if you think you are somehow immune from the psychological and emotional consequences of that brutality, because you did not suffer as they did and because you have a BMW in the garage, you are mistaken.

You may have thought you could stay sane by doing what you've always done, working hard, fitting in, and being "well spoken," but this strategy is taxing. You're so tired, on most days, you've almost given up on having the life you want and deserve. It's just easier to accept the day-to-day grind than fight for a bigger vision. You've quietly accepted defeat. Family responsibilities are exhausting enough, but add on top of that microaggressions at work and endless acts of overt racism and violence in the news.

There are levels to emotional pain. Things start out as frustrating and perhaps a bit uncomfortable, but manageable. Before you know it, you're taking Benadryl to help you sleep. What you really need is to manage what's keeping you up at night. Even if you generally think *I'm fine*, there are occasions when you have felt that life would be easier if you didn't wake up. You're probably not overwhelmed in every aspect of life but perhaps in more aspects than you would like.

Before the struggles of life get too far under your skin and too deep into your mind, take them out or they will take you out. First, you have to assess the problem and then use specific tools to neutralize the problem. That's not to say that issues won't still come up. In fact, you have to get to task on your well-being in part because, if you've learned nothing about the aftermath of George Floyd's murder, the non-prosecution of those who killed Breonna Taylor, and the racists who killed Black people while praying in a South Carolina church and shopping for groceries in Buffalo, New York, racism isn't going anywhere anytime soon.

You have so much to accomplish, but you truly are tired and overwhelmed. Added to that are the people around you who innocently remind you how "strong" you are and how impressed they are by all you have accomplished and how "put together" you always are. You don't want to disappoint anyone by switching things up (even when they are weighing you down).

Your circumstances are frustrating because you did what you were supposed to do: "earned good grades, went to college, started a respectable career to make good money." Why is long-lasting joy out of reach? It feels confusing at times.

You have a great sense of humor, but jokes will get you only so far. It's time to get to know yourself better but with grace and tenderness.

Imagine self-care that actually works. Yes, massage is amazing for stressed muscles. Pedicured toes are always lovely. But these are short-term solutions. As soon as you leave the masseuse's office or even their table, you're back to your worries and your woes. Imagine waking up on most mornings with an exciting new idea and fresh energy to carry it out. It's a novel idea, yes? What if you can shift your mind so even the benefits of your usual self-care strategies go further and last even longer? When you go to happy hour, you don't even need as many "dranks" or those three slices of cake because you aren't as depleted as you used to be. Imagine that. This is what high psychological fortitude can look like for you.

Somewhere deep in you a well of inspiration is available. You must first, however, tap into your psychological fortitude. *The Unapologetic Workbook* will show you just what to do. It will walk you through skills and strategies to undo some of your old habits so you can build new ones. It does so in a way that gently removes those habits, recognizing there is a reason they exist in the first place.

You already have resources that you can leverage to improve your daily life. Those skills have helped you. It may be time to reconfigure them for this stage of life. Using the workbook, you'll make better use of the strengths that are already in you.

Another novel benefit of this workbook is that it helps you preempt situations that would otherwise compromise your psychological fortitude. So many of us exist on a hamster wheel of life not recognizing how to get off the wheel. This workbook offers strategies to prepare for "war" in the time of peace.

You may have figured out that you need to do more to invest in your well-being. You need specific strategies to apply to your life. You know that there must be more to life than "this." This workbook provides new insight to your struggles and guides you through them to develop solutions just for you.

Whether you read and have highlighted every other sentence of *The Unapologetic Guide to Black Mental Health* or didn't read or listen to any of it and have no idea where you're supposed to begin, this workbook will get you on your way. It makes use of reminders from *The Unapologetic Guide* to affirm what you already know about racism, family stress, the daily grind, and burdens of life. But more importantly, it leans into psychological fortitude, recognizing that you can anticipate and prevent serious mental health problems by being proactive about your mind and your well-being.

The workbook accomplishes all of this by guiding you to identify stressors that you didn't know were so burdensome because you've been carrying them so long. Routinizing how you manage your stress will make it easier to manage unexpected troubles. The workbook also helps you better understand anxiety and depression, the two most common types of psychological challenges, so you can manage the strain that goes with them.

Here, I'll show you how to facilitate a reset of your mind to neutralize negative internalized messaging about being Black. You'll also gain specific insight for how to set boundaries that will strengthen relationships with your friends, family, and those who matter—all for the betterment of your psychological fortitude.

You will find that the ease of the work will come from accessing your spiritual compass. As you do so with each chapter of the workbook, you will achieve increasing psychological fortitude and lasting peace and joy despite whatever is happening around you.

Through this workbook, I want to meet you where you are to break down your mental health status in a way that makes sense. It doesn't matter so much that I earned a PhD, trained as a clinical psychologist, published more than sixty scientific papers, and became an award-winning professor and fellow in the American Psychological Association. It doesn't matter as much that I wrote the acclaimed *The Unapologetic Guide to Black Mental Health*. What matters most is how I understand the "rules" of being Black, the particulars that go with that identity, and the accumulated unaddressed pain in the community—pain that can be extracted beginning with you.

I learned the rules even when I wasn't supposed to be listening to grown folks' conversations. And then I collected the most helpful parts of traditional psychology and merged them with our cultural strengths to create a game plan for overcoming hardened emotional pain. You don't need fixing. You are part of multiple generations that have been adapting as needed...to survive. Unfortunately, adapting to a broken system that allows your employer to pay you less for doing the same work as a white colleague, that has no accountability for unfair treatment, and that seemingly sanctions African American death via legal and health care systems will eventually break you.

Otherwise, you're understandably numb and unable to access your entire mind. Unfortunately, we need you and your mind intact to advance a community that has been an underdog for too long.

This workbook embraces Black culture unapologetically and without the filter that suggests Black people are inferior, when truly Black people are brilliant and downright magical.

To be sure, doing the exercises will alleviate much of your emotional difficulty. However, it is unlikely to get to the heart of severe trauma symptoms, whereby you avoid certain places and doing certain things or suffer from nightmares and anxiety that sometimes accompany an abusive relationship, serious car accident, military combat, or witnessing the violent death of a loved one. Severe trauma will require seeing a professional who is trained in evidence-based interventions, such as cognitive processing therapy. You may try other interventions, keeping in mind that different approaches work for different people.

Black folks have dealt with mind-dysregulating realties for generations. What has accompanied this dysregulation is understandable apprehension about pursuing professional mental health care. Many experienced *The Unapologetic Guide to Black Mental Health* as a mix of inspiration and "Now what do I do?" Whether you read that book or not and whether you are in therapy or thinking about therapy, this workbook is for you.

CHAPTER 1

Your Psychological Fortitude (PF) Rating

You picked up this workbook as an indication of your readiness to be intentional about your emotional health and well-being. You recognize that your mindset and sometimes unpredictable emotions have been holding you back, but you are ready to get yourself to where you want to be in life.

This may be an unexpected place to begin, but stay with me for a moment. If you never use sunscreen or only use it on occasion, I want you to begin your journey by thinking about how SPF, or sun protection factor, works. Of course, you can get by without it, but the reality is that it is recommended to protect you outdoors from harmful UVB rays that cause cancer. It is true that we are less likely than white people to be diagnosed with skin cancer, but when we do get it, we are more likely to die from it. (That's another story for another time.) SPF protection is assigned different number values, such as SPF 15 or 50. The crude reason for the SPF number is that it tells you how long you can stay in the sun without burning when you are wearing a certain level of a product. Some people, depending on skin type, need higher SPF than others.

Sunscreen is sometimes waterproof, but after a while, it has to be reapplied to be effective. If you spend an extended amount of time outdoors, you may forget to maintain your protection. This happens when you are distracted with all the things that you need to do, like keeping an eye on your kids, brainstorming what you're going to have for dinner, rehashing an odd morning conversation, or working on your side hustle. And the hours slip by without you intentionally applying the protection you need from the sun.

This is also true for you regarding your "PF," or psychological fortitude, needs.

In life, we get distracted by other people's problems, worrying over family and planning for the next day. Too often, you are distracted by all the things you do for others rather than taking time for yourself—taking time to sit, reflect, and think about what is important and how you can re-up your psychological fortitude. However, renewing PF regularly is critical because we cannot rely on PF to take care of itself. We also cannot rely on the same level of effort that protected us during certain times of our lives to remain intact or be sufficient when our life circumstances shift with more and more demands. We must do things differently. And that is where this book comes in.

If you have picked this up and are willing to go through this journey with me, then you have some sense that you need a new approach to life to feel emotionally, spiritually, and physically healthy and to ultimately pursue your life purpose. Because your talents and gifts are so needed, I will do my best to help guide you. This journey is about learning to "reapply" your protections and also establish new protections. Life can be hard, especially if you are ill-equipped to manage the challenges that will come. Just like your melanin does not fully protect you from the sun, one boost to your PF (such as a single getaway with girlfriends or an inspirational Sunday church service) does not protect you from the serious and ongoing threats to your well-being. You'll need real skills and practice—luckily for you, that is what this book is all about.

This journey isn't just about living in lavish wellness—though I wish that and more for you! Black people in the United States and around the world (individually and collectively) need high psychological fortitude because we are faced with challenges that are pervasive and toxic for our minds. We face large-scale, systemic issues, like racism, discrimination, and inequity. Each of these—and we'll discuss this later—take an enormous toll on our mental health. The daily microaggressions and added imposter feelings or secret thoughts we have of being "less than" others fill our bodies with stress. Not to mention that getting the kind of quality care that can positively impact your PF is often expensive and out of reach for most folks. You need so much more than mental health or "well-being" in this era of invisibility and psychological warfare. You need an impermeable web of protection for your mind—and that protection is determined by your level of psychological fortitude.

What Is "Psychological Fortitude," and Why Is It Important to You?

I introduced "psychological fortitude" in my first book to motivate and empower anyone on this journey to not be distracted by the term "mental health." Of course, we all need mental health, but it has been hijacked by misinformation and assumptions that if you're not having a nervous breakdown, you're OK. This kind of stigma is proven by too many studies that show the majority of Black folks feel that mental illness is a sign of personal weakness.[1] Individuals who subscribe to that idea are misinformed.

I define "psychological fortitude" as your ability to take care of your work or school responsibilities, manage your emotions, take care of your physical health (especially if you have a chronic condition, like diabetes), and tap into your life purpose while also navigating the threats to your success. To me, psychological fortitude is about more than doing "OK." Doing OK can be a worthy goal. If you do the PF assessment that is coming up soon and you score low, getting to OK is the most worthy goal. For me, as someone who studies suicide in our community, I pray for those in crisis to have some normalcy and peace of mind. My mission is to help as many people as possible in the Black community to achieve that peace of mind and utmost psychological fortitude. If all of us were capable of that, I think our community deserves to celebrate.

But the real vision of this book is for you to find yourself in a position where you are able to experience life's joys, rebound from frustrations and negativity, and tap into your life purpose without being buried under the chaos of life. It is an important distinction. This isn't a book about making you robotically happy all the time. I want for you to be a fully actualized, unapologetic person; comfortable in who you are; capable of feeling sad but without getting stuck; and grateful to celebrate this messy, complicated experience of being alive. It is about feeling confident in who you are and what you want out of life and attaining a level of meaning and purpose that transcends the daily attacks of white American culture.

To use a car as a metaphor, your psychological fortitude is like the engine and the suspension. When it is high, it is pulling you forward, propelling you into whatever goals and ambitions you have, navigating through the world with voice-activated GPS. High PF makes it easy to take healthy risks because you feel confident that you can handle whatever comes at you and without getting too far off course. And, like the suspension, it also makes the ride smooth when you hit those inevitable potholes.

Keep in mind that your PF is not going to look like someone else's PF. PF is not one-size-fits-all. So you can stop looking around at your college roommate, your friends, and even your family. Instead, what you (or your loved one) need depends on a combination of how much exposure you have to life stress, relationship problems, family problems, financial struggles, and racism, and your internal state of mind and physical health, among other factors. Some people deal with life situations differently and can endure more than others. If you (or someone you care about) cannot take on as much as someone else, that does not make you either weak or crazy. You just have to prepare yourself differently and live your life unapologetically for you. Underline this: *You have to prepare yourself differently and live your life unapologetically for you.*

Checking Your Psychological Fortitude

So let's go ahead and rate your psychological fortitude. This is a metric we are going to come back to again and again throughout the book. The beauty of this simple system is that the rating doesn't have to be perfect, but it works for two reasons: (1) it's straightforward, and (2) it gives you an objective, numerical impression of where you are at one moment or on one day *relative to* another time. I highly encourage you to take at least one moment a day to check in with yourself and assign a PF rating. In seasons of high stress, you will have days that require you check in multiple times. Regardless, the exercise is ultimately about getting in touch with and observing yourself honestly. It is only when you begin making this a habit that you can do something when low ratings sneak up you.

Use the following psychological fortitude rating system as a quick self-check for how you are doing or when you want to check on someone else. I really like a 0-to-10 rating scale because you don't have to overthink it. You can do a quick evaluation and without a long list of questions or the alternative of saying you're "fine" or "blessed and highly favored" because that's what you say even when you're not doing so well.

- 10 means you feel phenomenal. Nothing and no one can break your spirit.
- 9
- 8
- 7 would pass as OK. You can recover from a very stressful day at work with just one glass of prosecco. You don't have the wherewithal to cook dinner, but you've had worse days and know that this too shall pass.
- 6
- 5 is the middle and less than ideal.
- 4
- 3 is not OK. You feel completely overwhelmed with life. If one more thing goes left, someone is going to catch hell. You have no idea how you ended up here and no way to get out.
- 2
- 1
- 0 would be lowest possible level of psychological fortitude. Your circumstances are bleak, you have zero desire to go on with life, and it's time to call someone you trust (or even text the crisis lifeline at 988) for help. *Don't think. Just reach out for help.*

Looking at the ratings and descriptions above and your capacity to manage your emotions, your responsibilities, and your purpose, despite everything that challenges you, you estimate. **My psychological fortitude rating is:** ______________. *Keep in mind that it doesn't have to be a perfect estimate but your best guess.*

Think about your rating in this moment. Take a moment to reflect on why you gave yourself the rating that you did.

____

____

____

Now, reflect on what you notice when assigning your PF rating. What kinds of experiences did you note when you thought of what your rating would be? Did you notice anything physical, like a sore jaw from clenching or butterflies in your stomach?

How about your mindset? Has there been a sticky thought or worry you can't shake?

If you have been replaying a scene or moment in your head that is distressing you, write it down.

Is work stressing you out? If yes, how?

How is your sleep? Do you have trouble falling asleep or wake up throughout the night?

Are you frustrated by how COVID has changed the way you enjoy life? Write how the pandemic has affected you.

____

____

____

Maybe there is a challenging relationship in your life that is taking energy from you. Write down a few sentences that describe this dynamic.

____

____

____

Just in case you weren't looking at your big picture the first time you answered, consider how you're doing once again. Quiet your mind and think to yourself as you respond. **My psychological fortitude rating is about:** ____________. *Remember, it doesn't have to be a perfect estimate but your best guess.*

Regardless of why, being open and kind to whatever rating you have is important. If you have a low rating, know that you didn't earn that rating. It did not seek you out. Instead, as you will learn on your journey, there are numerous ways that life chips away at our PF. Keep in mind there are no right or wrong answers in this workbook. There are only opportunities to unpack what is more or less helpful on your road to sustaining a higher PF.

Tracking Your PF

One of the best ways to get a sense of your PF is to take a longer chunk of time and simply track your score. This book will give you multiple chances to center yourself in the moment and take an honest look at how you're feeling. But another subtle skill is having a sense of your PF's history. Doing so can help you see patterns, like when your PF rating is consistently lower or higher. And how you can proactively protect your mind or schedule a PF-boosting exercise (more of those later in the book). So for this exercise, use the form below to track your PF over the course of the next week.

To do this, set a daily reminder for yourself. I like to use my phone for this. Then it can ping you as a reminder to check your PF. (If possible, try to check in at approximately the same time each day to establish a habit). After writing your rating, take a moment to reflect on how you feel and what might be impacting you. These can be loose notes; there's no need for full sentences.

Date	PF Rating (0–10)	Body Sensations	Mental Thoughts or Experiences	What's Affecting My PF?
Monday	*5*	*Tightness in my neck and shoulders. It feels hard to catch my breath.*	*I'm way too busy.* *I can't keep up.* *I'll never get everything done.*	*I desperately need to get a new job, but I don't have time because I'm overwhelmed with the job I have. I'm overworked and underappreciated at work* ***and*** *at home.*

Now that you've been tracking for a week, let's review your sheet. Were there any patterns you noticed? Such as specific days where your PF was lower or higher?

Any physical sensations that kept showing up?

Any surprises you discovered?

Anything else you noticed?

This tracker sheet can be tremendously helpful. Feel free to download a blank copy from http://www.newharbinger.com/50874 and use it as much as you like. Or create a journal prompt, if you use a daily journal, to keep track of your PF. As you'll see later, getting as much information as possible about your emotional health helps you stay on top of it. That's why this book is going to ask you to check in with your PF in each chapter, and I highly encourage you to make a daily habit out of it. You can check in the same time each day or along with the same activity, like at lunchtime or after dinner, to build your consistency.

What's Negatively Impacting Your PF?

After a week of tracking your psychological fortitude, I bet that you've begun to identify one or two things that may be regularly affecting you. So let's take a closer look at what all could be lowering your PF. Just like examining yourself to determine your PF, it is also important to figure out what may be impacting it. The short answer is that by looking at what may be undermining your PF, you can then explore ways to remove those PF-limiting circumstances. The result will be a higher PF. (And, as you will see later in chapter 3, you can also anticipate PF-harming challenges in life—a skill that may be useful for PF maintenance.)

What typically impacts our PF can be broadly labeled as "stress." Stress comes in lots of forms, but its impact on you, your mind, and your body is the same. In response to stress, our body releases the hormone cortisol, which, over time and in excess, has been shown to lead to all kinds of serious health problems. When we're chronically overwhelmed by stress, our mind can be conditioned to have too many negative thoughts that drag our PF downward. Many times, this alone can impact our PF. When we stew in our own internal dialogue—especially when its anxious or negative—our PF plummets. But often it's what we do in response to our thoughts and feelings that can supercharge our PF.

We all develop certain ways of handling stress. We often learn them from family members as we're growing up, or we can discover them on our own. Some strategies help us recover from and process stress, and others cause our PF to plummet. The trickiest kinds of stress-processing strategies actually feel good…for a minute. We finally get a break. But over time, these ways of coping with stress negatively impact our PF because they lead us to isolate ourselves or treat our body poorly.

Listed below are some common ways of reacting to stressful situations.[2] Circle those that you do or that you use frequently.

- I ignore my own needs and just work harder.
- I seek out friends for conversation and support.
- I eat more than usual or grab a bag of chips or other junk food.
- I engage in some type of physical exercise.
- I get irritable and take it out on those around me.
- I take a little time to relax, breathe, and unwind.
- I smoke a cigarette or drink a caffeinated beverage.
- I confront my source of stress and work to change it.

- I withdraw emotionally and just go through the motions of my day.
- I change my outlook on the problem and put it in a better perspective.
- I sleep more than I really need to.
- I take some time off and get away from my working life.
- I go out shopping and buy something to make myself feel good.
- I joke with my friends and use humor to take the edge off.
- I drink more alcohol than usual.
- I get involved in a hobby or interest that helps me unwind and enjoy myself.
- I take medicine to help me relax or sleep better.
- I maintain a healthy diet.
- I just ignore the problem and hope it will go away.
- I pray, meditate, and tap into my spiritual life.
- I worry about the problem and am afraid to do something about it.
- I try to focus on the things I can control and accept the things I can't.

Look back at the things you circled. (Some of them may have shown up on your tracker sheet.) The even-numbered items tend to be ones that maintain or boost PF, and the odd-numbered items tend to drain us over time when we use them to cope with stress. If you happened to check a few odd-numbered ones, it's OK. These are common strategies people use to cope with stress. The point here is that you now have a few areas that you can change immediately to balance things in your favor. The first steps on the journey to high PF are about removing self-limiting behaviors from your life. Start slow.

To make it easy, what's one thing you checked that you know is dragging you down. Try to pick something easy (and go easy on yourself).

___

Take a moment to think about why you use this strategy. How did you learn to do it? What makes it feel good in the moment?

____

____

____

____

____

Now, either look at the above list or think one up yourself. What is a more positive strategy you could use next time you're stressed and your PF is low?

____

____

____

Know also that just because what you've done in the past worked, it does not mean that it will always work. For example, running around on five hours of sleep worked when you were twenty-five years old. Now that you are forty-five, get some rest. You will have to continually evaluate whether what you are doing is working for you in life, or you will find yourself in a rut that is hard to escape. Don't assume that the same thing will always get you to where you need to be at every stage of life or life situation.

Exploring What High PF Looks Like

By the end of this book, I want you to have a more consistent experience of life with a high degree of psychological fortitude. People who have solid PF can cope with life stress, work more effectively, and recognize their purpose in life. You may have difficulty recognizing your life purpose because of unmanageable emotions or unrecognized and untreated depression. Because life happens, everyone benefits from high PF.

Let's imagine Angela as an example of what high PF looks like. Angela was a marketing director at a big firm. She graduated college with honors and spent the better part of a decade building her career. She was proud of her ability to support herself, but she started feeling empty, like she was just going through the motions of life. She could hardly identify what gave her joy anymore. It didn't help that she was tired of feeling undervalued at work when she knew that she was smarter and had better ideas than most of the senior executives at the firm. To add to all of that, her family was always asking when she was going to get married as if she could just choose a partner from a restaurant buffet.

Over time, her PF declined. She began to see that what she thought was helping her get through the stress of work and her family's opinionated questions was actually holding her PF back, causing her to spiral into binge-eating to deal with stress. She knew she wasn't herself and that she could do better.

After self-assessing, she was able to make small changes that slowly improved her PF each day, week, and month. Instead of the exhaustion she felt daily, she had a renewed energy that she then could spend on taking care of herself, eating better, developing a meditation plan, and scheduling time with friends.

When her PF was high (which wasn't all the time, but enough for her to feel more fulfilled), her mind felt focused and energized. She could complete tasks before giving up too quickly. She found time and space to reconnect with seemingly small but important details, like journaling small moments of gratitude that connected her to the abundance she had around her and taking time to ger her hair done by her favorite stylist. When a big task was due at work, she'd anticipate the workload and plan a vacation for herself when it was over to reward her effort and de-stress. She still dealt with microaggressions at work, including new clients who questioned that she was the actual marketing director, but now she was confident enough to log complaints with HR and develop a plan for her side hustle and new career.

As you can see, Angela's higher PF didn't happen overnight. It was the result of practice, dedication despite setbacks, and confidence that she could get to her higher self. But her ability to get her PF higher means that you can also.

Imagine Your High PF

Take a moment to imagine yourself once you have completed this workbook. Write down three ways you imagine your life will be different with higher PF.

1. ____

____

____

____

2. ____

____

____

____

3. ____

____

____

____

After taking some time to imagine yourself with a higher PF, what are a few things you can do right now to set yourself up for success?

____

____

____

____

____

____

Finding Your Guiding Light

To increase your PF, you're going to need commitment. Consider how Angela was able to stay on track long enough to flip her low PF. Before she committed to getting back on track, she felt alienated from the things that really mattered to her. For her, the signal that kept her on track was how she felt when she was being, and honoring, her true self. This came from knowing her values. We all have values. Some of them are personal and unique. Others we learn from our upbringing. Regardless, values that are honest and authentic for you are allies on your journey to a high PF.

By values, I mean your most deeply held principles of living. Your values are yours and yours alone. They are your personal beliefs about the way you want to live your life and what you want to stand for in your life. Here are some examples of values statements:

- I share my knowledge with other people to improve my community.
- I am a loving, kind, responsible parent for my children.
- I am a spiritual being who honors all forms of spirituality in others.
- I am a loving, compassionate, and supportive life partner.
- I am someone who keeps their word.
- I continually challenge and improve myself as a person.
- I maintain a plant-based diet for my health.
- I contribute to my community by performing acts of charity and volunteerism.
- I work to improve the lives of people who are economically challenged.
- I promote my physical and mental health until I am old.
- I protect the Earth and promote a clean, sustainable planet.
- I am available for my loved ones in their time of need.

So, what are some of your values? List a few of them here. Or write them in the notes app in your phone or on a piece of paper that you can put somewhere you'll see often.

1. I am/want to be ________________________________.
2. I am/want to be ________________________________.
3. I am/want to be ________________________________.
4. I am/want to be ________________________________.
5. I am/want to be ________________________________.

Values are your guiding light. When you get in touch with your values, they can provide motivation for change even in the midst of low PF. Values are a mental fuel that can propel you on the path toward a higher PF and a life full of meaning. In almost any life situation, there is no position to take that is more empowering than standing for your values.

Wrap Up

I wish that it did not have to be the case that Black people must have some type of magical ability to do well. Until things change, however, this is the reality. Give yourself some grace and be gentle with yourself on this path to high PF. It is bound to be full of starts and stops. But this beginning will help. Yes, changing some of your old ways will help get you started. As will getting to know yourself and what you are carrying each day. If anything, I hope this chapter helps you stay in touch with yourself like you would a best friend.

In the next chapter, we will dig more into self-care and how you can use it to boost your PF. Now that you are on your path, let us reinforce our individual and collective PF, and get clear about where you are, and more importantly, where you are going.

CHAPTER 2

Protect Your PF by "Re-Thinking" Self-Care

You had expectations for your life and what it was going to look like. Some of the expectations were driven by what your family expected and what they or others and society called "success," but they were expectations that you internalized for yourself nonetheless. In high school, you had plans to go to college, get your business or law degree, get married, and have your perfect son and daughter by the time you were thirty years old (and definitely by now). You did not expect that it would be so hard to save money to start your business. Of course, you had to start working right out of college so you could pay back those student loans. Now you are almost thirty or forty or fifty or sixty years old and feeling like *What's the point?* Everyone around you seems to be doing *way better* than you are. They are so happy with their lives that they could not imagine that you could be so miserable. No one would believe that there are days you have fleeting thoughts of some type of accident just to get some relief from your misery. You go to church and read Bible scriptures, but feeling better is always temporary. The dating scene is pitiful. The men that you meet have no capacity for conversation. You could stand to lose a few pounds, but you still cute. The universe must be plotting against you. You wonder why you just can't be happy like everybody else. This is what low psychological fortitude sounds like.

If only you had a mentor or more people who believed in your vision. It seems you have wasted time. Life just hasn't been fair. And as a result, you feel down and moody on more days than you care to say. Let's face it, if you are picking up this book, then your PF is lower than you would like. Or even if it is a good day and you are flying high, something unexpected can happen that is a threat to your PF. Either way, at some point in time, you are going to need emergency tools to keep your head above water and from relenting to the cycles of anxiety and depression. Self-care might be your life raft in these moments.

Before we start our self-care journey, let's check in on your PF in this moment. Take a few deep breaths. Quiet yourself for a second. And write down your current (0–10) psychological fortitude below.

PF rating (0–10): ________

I'm sure you've heard people talk about needing self-care as if it were any activity that makes them feel good. Audre Lorde likened self-care to self-*preservation* and insisted it was an act of political warfare for you to preserve yourself. Imagine that—in a world that has diminished you in so many ways. You preserving yourself might be antithetical to the establishment. Because self-care can take you to unimaginable heights, you want to be clear about what it can look like for you.

There are many things self-care is and many things it isn't. Self-care can be indulgent like a diamond-dust pedicure or full-body massage, but it doesn't have to be. It can rarely ever be self*ish*-care as some might say. It can definitely be used after a low moment to boost your PF higher or (as we'll learn in this chapter) preventatively to allow upcoming tough times to roll off your shoulders and at any time in between. Self-care is also more than a simple salon day or happy hour. At its best, it is an intention to treat your mind with respect, fill it with positivity, and expand your resilience to life hassles.

Self-care, whatever that is for you, is an essential tool in your struggle to keep PF high. Looking back at your PF rating above, if it is 6 or lower, I highly recommend you schedule some "me time" for yourself. (We will look into this in a bit.) If it was lower than a 3 and you are not quite ready to see a licensed mental health professional, then the first step on your journey is actually to take a few things off your plate.

The Power of Saying No

I know full well how hard it can be to say no. Perhaps you spent hours working on your son's school project the night before it was due. Perhaps you were on the phone all night with your sister trying to problem-solve her custody situation with her ex-husband. Just last week, your brother was in jail and needed you to go get him out. Maybe you were handling all of this just fine. But more than likely, you're like a frog in a pot of cool water sitting on a fire. The temperature will slowly increase, and you find that you are cooked before you know it. Even if you do show up for that next thing, you know deep down that you're too tired to even really be there fully.

The first thing you are going to need to practice is setting a boundary that communicates how much you value your sanity and make good on your commitment to reclaim your mind: saying no.

Calling In Black

There are times—and you know the ones I am talking about—when you might not know what you want to do self-care-wise, but you sure know you need to take something off your plate for a day. The workplace, especially if you are the only Black person or the only Black woman in your office, is a huge source of stress and anxiety for many of us. Some of us didn't realize how stressful the workplace was until the COVID-19 pandemic and we dreaded going back face-to-face.

"Evelyn from the Internets" introduced this phenomenal idea in one of her most popular YouTube videos, "Call in Black." (If you didn't already enjoy her videos before she took a hiatus, search for her YouTube channel or try this link: http://www.youtube.com/watch?v=cpVeUVcFMAU.)

When you are not feeling physically well, you call in sick so you can feel better and return to work with the capacity to get your job done. In the same way, when you are overwhelmed by the reality of navigating racism in our society, you can call in Black so you can stay home to stop your head from spinning or at least not worsen it with the fatigue of racism—racism to which few others (if any) in your office can relate.

You do not need an excuse to take care of your well-being. The totality of your many responsibilities can weigh on you more than you can bear. Let's make a deal: If you are holding on to all your paid time off for a rainy day, don't. If you are someone who loses your sick time at the end of the year, stop. Call in Black. Being Black is hard work.

For this exercise to work though, you need to be checking on your psychological fortitude (PF) each morning, at minimum, like we practiced in chapter 1, but you can also begin to track it throughout your waking hours. With your tracking, have an understanding of what you will do if your PF gets to be too low:

Date: ______________________________

My morning PF rating: ________

My midday PF rating: ________

My bedtime PF rating: ________

I, ______________________, promise myself that if my PF is under a 4, for more than two days in a row, that I will call in (Black or whatever you need to tell yourself) for work and get the rest I deserve.

After a while, life challenges add up. Everyone has a tipping point. It says nothing bad about you if you take some time for yourself. Taking time for yourself is *your most important responsibility*. Don't let the habit of putting yourself last get so entrenched that you forget why you do it.

When you have called in for the day, take a moment during that day off from work (or some other obligation) to answer the following questions, *honestly*.

What was it like to say no to one or more of my obligations today?

____

____

____

What did I do with my time?

____

____

____

What thoughts did I have about the kind of person I am or what it says about me for taking a day off?

____

____

____

Did my PF increase or decrease over the course of the day? What accounts for the change in my PF?

____

____

____

Hopefully, your PF rating improved simply because there was less pressure on you. You got some relief because you took control of your day and your time rather than being at the mercy of your job. Some of us, however, are embarrassed and confronted with painful negative thoughts of unworthiness and guilt when we do something as simple as say no. We will talk about this kind of thinking at the end of the chapter. It can sabotage self-care before you even get out the gate! But for now, just focus on your shoulders feeling a bit lighter in this moment.

Of course, work isn't the only place where you might have to say no. There are so many family and extended family obligations, sorority and frat demands, nonprofit engagements, and other occasions that take effort and where we need to be our full selves. But the power of saying no truly shows up strongest when we make a practice of it, temporarily removing draining activities from our days so we recover.

Take a moment to think of as many of your regular and routine tasks on any day as you can. From taking and picking your kids up from school to getting food for your homebound uncle to the endless Zoom meetings. List as many as you can.

1. ____________________
2. ____________________
3. ____________________
4. ____________________
5. ____________________
6. ____________________
7. ____________________
8. ____________________
9. ____________________
10. ____________________

Now go back through your list of daily responsibilities and rate each entry from 1 to 5, with 5 being a PF-draining activity. If you rated any a 5, explore how you might be able to say no to that activity tomorrow—or, in a best case, say no permanently. Life is never perfect, but brainstorm a few ways you could say no to one of these.

____

____

____

Keep in mind that saying no can look like many things. It isn't all cut and dry, like "I'm calling in Black" on this forever. If picking up your kids every day is the straw that breaks your back, saying no might look like exploring carpool options or having another mom trade off days for pickup if possible. This is how we build community.

Now That You're Saying No, What Do You Want to Say Yes To?

If you're like me and you called in Black to work today, you may be left with a strange feeling of *What do I do now?* It is rare that this amount of time is now free. And the void left behind can feel a little daunting. That's why it's good to be clear about what fills your cup. That way you don't have to think too hard or too long. It'll be tempting to take on something that ends up being stressful.

What Fills You Up?

Self-care is all about balancing the scales and making sure you are pursuing the same amount of restorative, pleasurable living as you are facing challenges.

Look at the list below and check any activities that typically fill your cup.

- Take a nap when you find yourself with an unscheduled hour or two.
- Pick up some fresh flowers and display them where you'll see them most often.
- Get delivery from one of your favorite restaurants or treat yourself to a fancy dinner out because you've earned it.
- Instead of always going to the tried-and-true, try a new restaurant this week. You might discover a new go-to.
- Create a playlist of your favorite five songs from back in the day.
- Learn the basics of a new language.
- Go to a comedy club or watch a special on TV. Laughter really is the best medicine.
- On a sunny afternoon, grab a folding chair or blanket and your favorite tea or other beverage, go to a park, stare up at the clouds, and let your mind wander from big to small thoughts.
- Go for a bike ride or a drive to nowhere in particular.
- Attend a local music performance. Many small clubs, restaurants, and coffee shops have free admission for shows.
- Listen to a chapter or two from an audiobook.
- Allow yourself to sleep in a couple of extra hours this weekend; errands and chores can wait!
- Next time you're getting lunch, buy lunch for the person behind you in line. Say you're "paying it forward" and walk away with a smile on your face.

- Reserve a night at a hotel outside of town, somewhere you've never spent much time. Explore the scene and enjoy the sights or stay inside and read a new book.
- Listen to a podcast on an unsolved mystery.
- Make a list of three bucket list places you might like to visit and research things to do in those places for when you go one day.

Looking at the things you checked off the list above, pick three or write three of your own that can form the basis of a regular self-care routine. Think of things you can do each week (or every other week at minimum) if possible.

1. ______________________________
2. ______________________________
3. ______________________________

Self-Care for the Future

It's crucial for your PF that you regularly and routinely do self-care. Little things each week that fill you up have tremendous power in incrementally increasing your PF because they are the spice that makes life worth living. But as it is with life, sometimes things get in the way.

Now, I'm not talking about surprises. I am talking about moments that you know are coming, that you might be dreading. Well, it turns out self-care can protect your PF a little bit if you decide to solidify your mind before you take on a challenge. Trust me—it's best to build yourself up as high as you can when you know that there is something over the horizon that could leave you bruised.

Prepare for War in the Time of Peace

Take a moment to think over your next week or month. If you keep a calendar, take a look at it. Zero in on an event or task that you *know* is going to take a lot out of you—the kind of thing that makes you tense just thinking about it.

Stressful event: ______________________________

Event date: ______________

This is going to take a little bit of planning, but stick with me here. In the days leading up to your stressful event, what self-care can you do to make sure you are well rested and emotionally well going in to it? Brainstorm three things.

1. ______________________________

2. ______________________________

3. ______________________________

Try to think of things that are a little bit extra from your routine self-care list. Maybe it's a drive to a beautiful beach or lake for a few hours. Or a dinner-date night with girlfriends or your partner. Maybe it's a massage. Whatever your ideas are, make sure they restore you just a little bit extra. Put at least two on your schedule. Book them now if you have to. Your PF will thank you later.

Just Breathe

The self-care we've been exploring up until now has really been about lifestyle changes when you are feeling worn-out and tired or know that there is an upcoming challenge. The rituals that we do to build our PF are very important to our overall well-being. The best ones are activities that allow us to reset our minds and relax our bodies so we feel whole and rested.

However, there are times, and I'm guilty of this too, when it is hard to enjoy the self-care moment. Our minds tend to zoom off into all of tomorrow's hassles or past traumas. This hijacks our enjoyment of the moment. When this happens, it's important to have micro-self-care tools to cease the endless chatter and give you a moment to experience the restorative power of whatever it is that brings you joy.

But let's face it, our heads are full of clutter most of the time anyway. And so the next practice is also super helpful in the throes of a low-PF moment too.

You Already Breathe, Just Breathe Deeper

Breathing deeply is one of the simplest, but most important, things that you can do to increase psychological fortitude. It is simple because you can do it anywhere. There are only two things that can limit its effectiveness.

1. **Trying to do it "perfectly."** Because you have to retrain your breathing, the overachiever in you will be so focused on getting it "just right" that you will overthink it and perhaps berate

yourself for not getting it right. If you struggle for perfect breathing, you will have already missed the point of the activity.

2. **Remembering to do it at crucial moments.** A crucial moment is when you are overwhelmed, do not know what to do, and need to put yourself in mental timeout before you make a decision or do something that will not help you in the long run.

Breathing deeply takes you out of the moment when you are most stressed about what is happening around you and transports you to a safe place. Oftentimes, we just need to be removed from a situation in order to gain a fresh, and perhaps different, perspective on what's going on.

Deep breathing is also good for your health because it helps your body's stress response, which is regulated by your sympathetic and parasympathetic nervous systems. When you are overwhelmed by stress, your heart rate increases and your blood pressure rises, both responses of your sympathetic nervous system. Some have likened it to the gas pedal in your automobile. Press the pedal and all systems go! It is a natural response to stress that can become unnatural if you experience ongoing unmanaged stress. Breathing deeply allows the parasympathetic nervous system to be activated like a brake pedal, which calms you down and refreshes your view. You are forced to do something that most adults are bad at doing for the body—slow down to take oxygen into the body appropriately.

Think about when your doctor tells you to take a deep breath. You do so like a good student (or so you think). Your superman chest expands and lifts as far as you can get it to go. However, deep breathing is not about expanding your chest. It is about breathing from your belly. Deep breathing is about getting oxygen in your body directed where it is supposed to go. If you ever notice a baby in a crib, her little belly looks like it has a balloon in it that cycles from inflating to deflating over and over again. This is how we as adults are supposed to breathe, but we have gotten lazy with our breathing over time. When you have a moment to put the book or your app down, put one hand on your chest and one hand on your tummy, and take a deep breath. Which moved more? Your chest or your tummy? You want your tummy to move more.

Track Your Breathing

There is going to come a time when you are with your whole family for a big event or traveling to your hometown for a wedding, holiday, or funeral. All the usual suspects are there. You love your family, but being around all of them at the same time is just too much. Deep breathing helps manage your reactions and protect your PF. Maybe you need to use your deep breathing more often than just big family occasions. You have to go to that job of yours where you are the only Black woman as far as the eye can see. Maybe you are out doing something you love, but you encounter an unexpected "Karen." When any difficult moments arise, even when you happen upon your nemesis in the elevator, take a deep breath. Try it out for a week. Use the following tracking sheet to note when you took time to breathe deeply and how you felt afterward.

Date and Time	Event, Obstacle, or Crisis	Duration of Deep Breathing	Your PF Afterward (0–10)

If you prefer a video tutorial for deep breathing, you can find one I did on YouTube at http://youtu.be/BCgrY3MPC7U. If my example doesn't work for you, there are different approaches, so find one that walks you through methods that work best for you. Your goal is to be able to focus on your own body and your own breathing. Practice is what will help you remember to take a deep breath in the midst of life's stressors. Keep in mind also that first noticing tension in your body could be a good prompt to practice.

Look back at your tracker sheet for the last week. What do you notice?

____

____

____

____

____

Were you able to practice daily deep breathing?

____

____

____

____

____

If so, how often did it help how you felt?

____

____

____

____

____

If it was hard to remember to do it, how did the few times go when you did breathe deeply? Or, if not, what kept you from practicing?

____

____

____

____

____

Eliminate Thinking Traps

Now that you are using deep breathing to stop stress in its tracks, you may have noticed how good it is at "braking" against some thoughts or interrupting the negative things you tell yourself. Hopefully, over a week of paying attention, you noticed how your running thoughts take a break when you pause to breathe in a deeper way. This is a related phenomenon the breathing gives us—a moment of relief.

Sometimes though, breathing isn't enough because our minds have gotten really powerful at giving us the business, especially negative ideas about ourselves. And no amount of breathing may help excessive worrying or dwelling on the past—or those all-present thoughts of unworthiness, shame, and failure. So in addition to breathing, you are going to need extra tools to quit these thoughts. This is especially true if you want to develop higher PF. These types of negative thoughts are found time and time again in people who have elevated anxiety and depression, and studies have shown that these issues become worse when you devote time and energy to believe them.

So let's go through three common thinking traps that get in the way of our self-care or simply hijack our minds. The key to these exercises is to incorporate your breathing practice first to clear the way and then proceed.

Negative Thinking Trap 1: Expectations and "Shoulding" Yourself

If I could, I would absolutely remove the word "should" from every dictionary. Its only purpose is to highlight a "failure" that exists in your mind and to make you feel bad. Think about it. You say "should" to motivate yourself to do something you haven't done. You might say, "I should eat healthier," or "I should work on my business plan." It may very well be true that eating better and working on your business plan are your goals, but if you have not been doing either, I am sure that there is a good reason. Maybe you do not eat better because you need to plan your meals and go to the grocery store to prepare those meals. If you have not made time for either of these tasks, how are you going to eat better? Saying that you "should" only makes you feel worse because you are doing the best that you can with, let's say, your limited time and options.

You rack up double distress points when you should on other people. You say things like, "They *should* call and check on me sometime." "My girlfriend *should* cook for me." "My husband *should* help me out more around the house." "Given all that I do for my family, they *should* appreciate me more." These are just a handful of examples of how shoulds do nothing but make you resentful, angry, and stressed that you aren't doing enough or that something isn't happening the way you would like.

Stop "Shoulding" on Yourself

If you can, think of someone you trust to be honest with you and not judge you. They could be a close friend, partner, or family member. The key is that you trust them enough to be vulnerable because you are going to ask them to help you out. Next time you talk with them, either ask them to track what you say or simply get them to recall any and all of the "shoulds" you use. Bonus points if they write them down as you talk. I encourage you to pay attention to how you use the word "should." See if you can write your ten most common "shoulds."

1. ______________________________
2. ______________________________
3. ______________________________
4. ______________________________
5. ______________________________
6. ______________________________
7. ______________________________
8. ______________________________
9. ______________________________
10. ______________________________

As far as I am concerned, there is no reason for you to ever use it. It will take time, but you can remove it from your vocabulary because it will just make you feel bad. Usually, you can replace "should" with "it would be helpful."

- It would be helpful if my spouse cleaned the kitchen more.
- It would be helpful if I can get my business plan together.
- It would help me feel less frustrated with all that I have to do if my family appreciated what I do accomplish.

This simple language change removes the guilt from what you or someone else is not doing. I find it hilarious that, when I talk to an audience about removing the word "should" from their vocabulary, someone ends up using it in a question or comment right away. Some have an immediate awareness, while others wonder why members of the audience are chuckling. We have no idea how ingrained our use of "should" is, along with its negative expectations. So please, do not try to remove the word right away. Just be aware of it, if possible. The first step is to recognize the problem.

So take five of your "shoulds" and try to reframe them as "It would be helpful if..."

1. ______________________________
2. ______________________________
3. ______________________________
4. ______________________________
5. ______________________________

The next step is to rewrite the sentences above, but at the end, write an acceptance statement that gives you time to restore and reclaim your mind. Like this:

"It would be helpful if I can get my business plan together, but I am OK with not pressuring myself to do that right away because I need to rest a little first. My business plan will be better off if I take some time for myself."

Now you try.

1. ______________________________
2. ______________________________
3. ______________________________

4. ______________________________

5. ______________________________

Lastly, it helps to problem-solve other obstacles that have kept you from achieving one task that is important to you. You might say, "It would be helpful if I get my business plan together, so I need to search for free services for small business planning and also set aside one hour on the weekend and twenty minutes on weeknights to research this." Try it for one of your statements here.

____

____

____

____

____

____

____

Negative Thinking Trap 2: Useless Thinking vs. Useful Thinking

We all *interpret* what situations mean or what we think happened especially when other people are involved. Unfortunately, we miss part of the story in many situations because we don't have access to the whole story—in fact, we rarely know the whole story! Remember the waitress who treated you poorly the other day? You paid good money for your food but couldn't know she was distracted by a sick child or mother at home.

We can all work to improve how we see ourselves and the people around us in ways that support our PF. Psychologists and other mental health professionals call this work "cognitive restructuring." The goal is to change your stressful thinking and replace it with a less stressful way of seeing everyday situations. Your mother might argue, "But I know she saw us," when her friend ignored you in the shopping mall, and you might insist, "I know that waitress was acting funky because she didn't want to serve us." Both could be true. The question is, is it worth your psychological fortitude to be right, or could you assume that you might be missing part of the picture? In the interest of not letting the situation rob you of enjoying a lovely meal or rob your mom of special time with her grown daughter, choose the self-talk that supports your peace of mind.

There are a number of ways that we interpret situations and then talk to ourselves as if our interpretations are fact. In the end, it's less than helpful but happens all the time. Despite all of your success—winning in corporate America, moving hearts and souls in entertainment, and managing households where everyone seems to be in their right mind—your useless thoughts persist.

The key is to interrupt the process. Breathing certainly helps as a starting point, but for your unhelpful thinking, the best protocol is to turn the thought over in your mind, see if it serves you or if it is helpful in any way, and replace it with another thought that is more helpful. Put another way, it looks like this:

Step 1. Notice it. One clue to a deeply ingrained useless thought is that you "feel a certain way about it" or you feel a certain way before you even think it.

Step 2. Acknowledge it for what it is: useless negativity. You could be right about your thought, but does being right help your PF in this context? Honestly?

Step 3. Have a little chat with the negativity inside your head. You have permission to evaluate what is most important. Do you prefer to assume that your thought is correct and sabotage your own well-being? Or do you want to explore other options? Begin by thinking of what else might be true or let go by assuming there are things you don't know about the situation.

Step 4. Replace it. Decide that you want optimal psychological fortitude for yourself. Replace your negative talk with more positive ways of thinking about your world and the people around you. This is a skill that is built up gradually moment by moment, thought by thought. So keep at it.

Let's try it out. Sometime during your day, if you find yourself thinking negatively, write the thought down here.

Notice it: ____

____

____

Then write a statement of acknowledgment for what this thought really is doing for you.

Acknowledge it: ____

____

____

Now evaluate the thought. Write down whatever comes to mind.

Evaluate it: ____________________

____

____

Choose your next moment. Explore what you can say to yourself instead that is more helpful and gives you something you can hold onto as you go about your day.

New alternative thought: ____________________

____

____

For a bit more practice, here are the steps again. Feel free to take any thoughts that come to you.

Notice it: ____________________

____

____

Acknowledge it: ____________________

____

____

Evaluate it: ____________________

____

____

New alternative thought: ____

____

____

Notice it: ____

____

____

Acknowledge it: ____

____

____

Evaluate it: ____

____

____

New alternative thought: ____

____

____

This process is always available to you. The crucial part is noticing the negative self-talk in the moment, breaking it down, and replacing it with something that builds you up and restores your psychological fortitude.

Wrap Up

You are at the beginning of your journey to a higher PF. It is really important to keep an eye on your stress levels. If you've learned anything in this chapter, I hope it is that you are not powerless when it comes to how stress affects you. Setting proper boundaries to uphold your PF by working through challenges, saying no when you need to say no, and taking time for yourself are the first crucial tools toward reclaiming your mind.

If you are finding yourself buried in negative self-talk or shoulding, these are signals that your stress is probably high. Give yourself a break. Begin the work of organizing and making space for your self-care. This process of filling your cup both in response to and anticipation of stressful events is going to help you maintain your PF. Get out and practice the breathing and thinking tools to prevent useless thinking from negatively impacting your stress and PF. And over time, I promise you that a life lived in commitment to self-care will raise your psychological fortitude.

CHAPTER 3

"Clutch" Skills for When Your PF Is Too Low

If you've been incorporating as much self-awareness and self-care as you can, you are hopefully starting to feel the momentum of a higher PF and how you feel when you are closer to your best self than when you are not. However, there are times when no matter how much attention you pay yourself, "life gets you down."

You may have experienced moments, days, or even weeks of profound and unaddressed low PF. These can be hard and challenging times. It's also possible that if you have persistently low psychological fortitude, the persistence is due to you having had a profoundly troubling life experience—an experience that you did not have the resources to manage at the time. This is why abuse and neglect that happen in childhood have so much impact for the remainder of our lives and can result in years of low PF. Your childhood was the most vulnerable stage of your life because you did not have the maturity to understand what was happening to and around you. Your undeveloped mind coped the best way that it knew how, creating narratives of who you were and what you deserved. Now that your mind has matured and has more problem-solving capacity, let's be intentional about maximizing your PF and reclaiming your mind.

Because every victory counts, congratulate yourself for grabbing this book when you needed to shift some things. You are fortunate that you can recognize when you are in the middle of a low PF "episode" and take it seriously so you can give yourself a break rather than berating yourself for not being able to push through it. Feelings of depression or anxiety, low mood, lack of interest in life, and maybe even the passing thoughts of being dead demand an emergency intervention.

These times of severe low PF are more common than you think. And they are likely exacerbated by anxiety or depression. These two often co-occur, meaning that approximately 50 percent of people who experience debilitating levels of anxiety will also suffer from symptoms of depression and vice versa.[3] In this chapter, we'll work through these emergency PF situations, so you can recognize anxiety and undo beliefs that you may hold, like the notion that worrying all the time is a normal part of being Black. We must begin to address important realities that have likely impacted you and the people you love—realities like how all of that worrying is making you physically ill and how you can choose to get professional help for debilitating anxiety. Many are unaware, but anxiety-related problems are the most commonly occurring problems in the United States. They are a real threat to your psychological fortitude.

Before we begin learning our clutch skills, let's check in on your PF. Take a few deep breaths. Quiet yourself for a moment. And write down your current psychological fortitude below.

PF rating (0–10): ________

What did you notice about your rating today?

____

____

____

What types of things may be impacting it negatively?

____

____

____

What types of things might be keeping your PF from being higher than it would have been in a similar situation in the past?

____

____

____

When Your PF Is Too Low

Imagine an African American mother who works full time and is very active in her community. At work, she is a supervisor who is responsible for multiple employees (and their difficult personalities). She is a good-hearted person who takes it all in stride. At home, she cooks meals, keeps the house clean, and makes sure that her children do their homework. She also makes sure that they get to their numerous extracurricular activities throughout the academic year, including sports on Saturdays. She is in church every Sunday and sometimes volunteers with one of the ministries. In the community, she holds office in two civic organizations.

As you might imagine, she is tired. She is also chronically stressed and sleep-deprived, as she lies awake at night for hours because she cannot fall asleep. She oftentimes has problems concentrating at work and no longer knows what gives her joy. When she stops to think, she feels tearful and sometimes wants to run away from it all. She could be depressed. She could also be managing a tremendous amount of anxiety. Though she does an impressive job of keeping everything together for appearances, the effort in doing so only adds to her stress. When she assesses her psychological fortitude honestly, she finds it very low: logging in at 3 to 4 on most days.

A lot of people experience very low PF, but do not recognize it as a problem. You may believe you're too strong to be overcome by emotional problems. Whether or not you acknowledge this temptation to view yourself as superhuman, it's important to know when there is a serious problem.

It is normal to feel anxious about a job interview or your kindergartener's first day of "real" school or pulling off opening night for a major production that you have been working on for weeks or months. A certain amount of *short-term* nervousness that includes physical symptoms like nausea or shakiness is to be expected from time to time. Anxiety that goes on and on and is out of proportion to a situation, keeping you from your life goals, is *not* good.

If you are honest with yourself, you will realize that you are so overwhelmed that it feels impossible to clear your mind even when you are in the shower. Really, when was the last time that you showered without thinking about what happened that day or what you needed to do the next day? If you don't remember, your memory lapse could be a sign of low PF.

Despite everything you worry about, you cannot get yourself mobilized to do anything differently in your life. It seems just enough to push your way through to get up each day. It does not feel good. That's what PF that is too low feels like.

We neglect our emotional health the same way that we neglect our physical health, except that our neglect for our emotional health is far worse. We neglect problems until the situation is dire or can no longer be avoided. If you were to break your arm, you would see a physician right away because achieving anything with a broken arm would be really hard to do. Because emotional problems do not shut us down right away, we keep going despite the potential long-term consequences.

Ongoing worry, feelings of emptiness, negative thoughts, inability to relax, lack of sleep, and excessive irritability are signs of diminished PF that warrant your attention. Do you find that the smallest thing will set you *off*? It happens to the best of us. Unfortunately, when you wait out your symptoms in hopes that they go away, even when they seem to disappear, there can still be a serious problem waiting to reemerge.

Maybe Anxiety Is Your Low PF Problem

Have you ever been told that you make up things to worry about? Even then, perhaps you cannot seem to get your worrying under control. Before now, you may have accepted it as "who you are," but anxiety is a serious speed bump along the way to achieving higher psychological fortitude.

If you can find anything to worry about on any given day, have a hard time being reassured about the thing or things that you worry about—even when you talk to others that you trust—and this has been your way of life for years, it may be that you have high anxiety.

Take a moment to answer the questions below.[4]

Are you troubled by the following?

☐ Yes ☐ No Do you worry about multiple areas of life, like your job situation, relationship/situationships, your children, and more?

☐ Yes ☐ No Is your worry excessive in how intense it feels, how often it happens, or how upset you get when you worry?

☐ Yes ☐ No Do you find it difficult to control the worry (or stop worrying) once it starts?

☐ Yes ☐ No Do you worry excessively or uncontrollably about seemingly little things such as being late for an appointment, minor repairs, homework, or other day-to-day situations?

Think about the topics you worry about most often excessively or uncontrollably. List them here.

☐ Yes ☐ No During the *last six months*, have you been bothered by excessive worries more days than not?

During the past six months, have you often been bothered by any of the following symptoms more days than not? If so, how much has it affected your daily life?

	Not at all		A little		Moderately		Quite a bit		Extremely
Restlessness or feeling keyed up or on edge	⓪	①	②	③	④	⑤	⑥	⑦	⑧
Irritability	⓪	①	②	③	④	⑤	⑥	⑦	⑧
Difficulty falling or staying asleep, restless or unsatisfying sleep	⓪	①	②	③	④	⑤	⑥	⑦	⑧
Easily fatigued	⓪	①	②	③	④	⑤	⑥	⑦	⑧
Difficulty concentrating or mind going blank	⓪	①	②	③	④	⑤	⑥	⑦	⑧
Muscle tension	⓪	①	②	③	④	⑤	⑥	⑦	⑧

How much do worry and physical symptoms interfere with your work, social activities, family, and other important areas of your life?

⓪	①	②	③	④	⑤	⑥	⑦	⑧
Not at all		Mildly		Moderately		Severely		Very Severely

How much are you bothered by worry and physical symptoms (how much distress do they cause you)?

⓪	①	②	③	④	⑤	⑥	⑦	⑧
Not at all		Mildly		Moderately		Severely		Very Severely

If you answered "severely" or "very severely" to any of these questions, chances are that you are struggling with anxiety. Anxiety is one of the most common mental health challenges and a saboteger of PF. But thankfully, it can be managed and is very treatable.

There are also physical symptoms of anxiety that you may have dismissed but are connected to what mental health professionals call "panic disorder." Have you ever unexpectedly had a racing heartbeat or the sense that your heart is skipping beats and shortness of breath, perhaps with a choking feeling? Some people feel in their mind that they are going crazy when this happens, but the feeling is so intense that they may have wondered if they needed emergency care. In fact, some people call 911 only for hospital staff and doctors to assure them they are in good health. Eventually, the scary feelings pass, and the once terrified person can recover.

Ruling out a serious health problem, like a heart condition, is important, but anxiety will not kill you. It can, however, severely undermine your PF. For diagnosis and accompanying intervention, see a mental health provider who uses evidence-based practices.

Let's Talk About Depression

What inspired me to earn a PhD was the assumption in mainstream psychology that Black people's depression looks the same as white people's depression. Many African Americans (or at least the ones who identify as African American) assume that Black people do things differently, see things differently, feel things differently, and even say things differently than do white people. Depression can also look different for us.

Dr. F. M. Baker described some of the unique ways we experience depression. She described the "detached long-sufferer" who proclaims that faith in God keeps them going despite the circumstances that weigh them down, and the "John Henry Doer" whose health is compromised by overworking but nevertheless persists in overworking and taking care of everything and everyone else but themselves.[5] Both are labels that apply for many African Americans who experience but don't acknowledge depression and find a way to "just keep it moving."

The data-supported research suggests that though a Black person and a white person might seem to have the same level of depression symptoms, the Black person will not acknowledge thoughts of suicide and may be more likely to acknowledge other depression symptoms, such as sleep problems.[6] Even still, they may also get out of bed and go to work every day and not miss a day for forty years. They may not "feel" depressed, but that does not mean that the depression is not there. It only means that the depression profile is different and thus more likely to fly under the radar. This is partly why I developed the idea of your daily psychological fortitude rating. It can often point to emergencies that aren't obvious.

Depression shows up in common ways, like feeling down all the time, but it also shows up as problematic thought patterns and traps, similar to the ones we combated last chapter. The example

I spoke of earlier in this chapter, about the very active, sleep-deprived supervisor-mom, is a good illustration of what depression can look like. If you are experiencing depression, you will also find yourself with thoughts that replay over and over in your mind and won't go away. These thoughts are broadly labeled as "rumination."

When your boyfriend makes plans without you on the anniversary of your first date and you replay over and over (in your mind only) why he would do such a thing, that is rumination. You are not going to come up with the answer to his poor planning on your own. Replaying that exasperating situation keeps you from communicating effectively and can worsen your mood. Rather than addressing the true source of the problem, you end up paralyzed with inaction and no solution. Rumination is not helpful and only serves to escalate anxiety and potentially depression. Can you recall a single occasion in which you felt better after you ruminated over a time that you were mistreated? Rumination is not a disorder, but a feature of both anxiety and depression. Rumination is happening when the negative thoughts in your head replay like a vinyl record that skips repetitively due to a scratch. Are you familiar with scratched records that would play the same annoying pop and skip until someone picked up the needle and moved it beyond the scratch? If you do not move the needle along, you end up in a perpetual state of anger and frustration.

Look at this list and circle any that have come up for you in the last two weeks.

- Spiraling negative thoughts about yourself or your future
- Finding it hard to tolerate feeling frustrated
- Waking up throughout the night or having difficulties falling asleep
- Loss of appetite or overeating
- Difficulties paying attention and concentrating
- A diminished sense of personal worth, self-doubts, and indecisiveness
- Loss of ambition and enthusiasm
- Loss of sexual desire
- Feeling sluggish or "out of it"
- Fatigue
- Easily irritated
- Suicidal thoughts

If you checked five or more of these, it is highly likely that your low PF is due in part to depression. Adhering to some of the self-care behaviors you established in the last chapter are going to help. If you are feeling depressed, your first steps are to get good sleep by turning off all screens one hour before bedtime, replace carbs and sugars with vegetables and fruits, spend more time outdoors and in the sun (if you can), and do anything that connects you to the values you wrote down in chapter 1. By using the thought exercises you practiced in the last chapter, episodes of depression will get more manageable. You may decide that seeking professional help is necessary. (Chapter 7 discusses how to prepare to see a professional, how to assess what's needed, and how to get help.)

The Struggle of Low PF Can Be Inherited

I am often asked, "Does mental illness run in families?" When you ask this question of me, I hear the disguised but detectable fear in the question. It sounds like an intellectual question, but the fear is heavy when you are thinking about your fourteen-year-old daughter or son.

The short answer to your fearful question is, "Yes, psychological problems can run in families." Serious problems, like schizophrenia, where the affected person has lost touch with reality, and bipolar disorder, when the person has erratic mood swings, are more likely to be inherited than other less-severe types of problems (like anxiety and phobias).

Psychologists and other mental health professionals ask about family history in an attempt to pinpoint the nature of your struggles and uncover the severity of your emotional health problems. It's not unusual to have a family history, but obviously, not everyone whose family has members with mental health problems will inherit the same types of disorders. Sometimes what people inherit is a *vulnerability* or a predisposition that is triggered by a stressful situation. They have a low tolerance for stress. When we say that problems run in families, we are more likely to see serious psychological problems in individuals when other family members (living or deceased) have or had such challenges.

The point of asking and discovering this is to relieve the pressure of thinking that you did something wrong and perhaps even to get ahead of escalating less-serious issues that go unaddressed and could turn into more serious problems. Your struggles are not something you created or are too exhausted to fight. Struggles with anxiety and especially more serious problems, like bipolar disorder, are not caused by your own actions, but are rooted in how your brain is wired to deal with the world around you. Since that environment involves our family and the relationships that made us who we are, it is a good idea to make a PF family tree to get a history of your PF's journey through those that came before you.

Making a Mental Health Family Tree

Use the chart below to write the names of your closest blood relatives. We love our play aunties and cousins, but think about your biological relatives, who they are and how they handle stress. If the family member has passed on, try to remember anything that you can about how they handled challenges in life. Was your grandfather often angry? Does your mom smoke two packs of cigarettes a day? The only data you need for this exercise is your memory or frequent stories you heard. Using the lens of psychological fortitude, see if you can identify if their PF was often high and why? Or low and why?

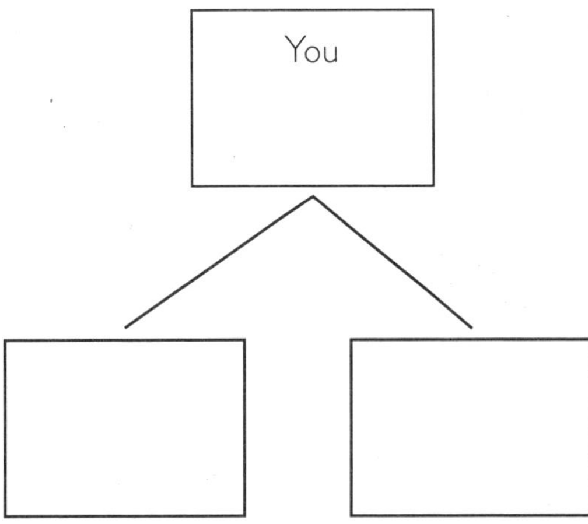

Figure 3.1

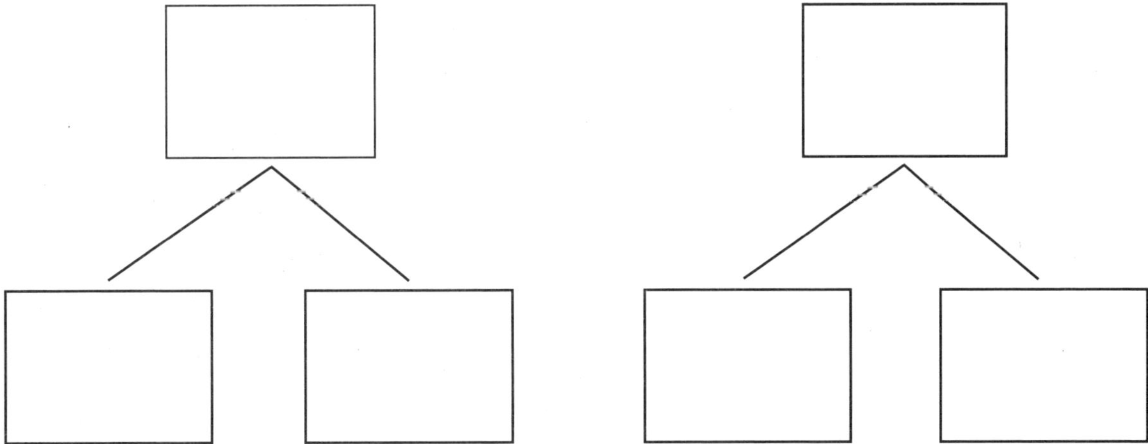

Figure 3.2

Looking at your family tree, is there anything you notice about behaviors that were problematic? Are there similarities, differences, or even patterns that you recognize in yourself?

____

____

____

Are there any family members who you felt had a high PF on most days? What are some things you can learn about how they tackled stress that may help you overcome low PF?

____

____

____

We will return to digging in our roots in a little bit. But the point here is that a lot of times, it didn't start with you. These challenges that decrease your PF rating are not your fault. And you need to look at them as such. Whether it is depression or bingeing alcohol, there is no shame in acknowledging these issues and tackling them head-on. We may not have the power to prevent them from coming for our PF, but we do have the power to change how we feel about the thoughts and feelings that come with them and strategies we use to manage them.

Clutch Skills for Low PF

When we have low PF, we are anxious, worrying, thinking about all the things that could go wrong in the future, and neglecting the very things that bring us joy. There are many skills and practices—from mindful meditation to cognitive and behavioral strategies—that have been proven to work. Below are a few of those skills.

When Your Worry Is Intense: Schedule Worry Time

It may seem backward, especially when worry is all it seems we can do. But for this exercise, I want you to set aside time exclusively for worry. This idea may seem strange because it runs counter to our usual instincts.

The truth is that worry thrives on our mind thinking it is "bad" to do. We try to resist worrying and end up escalating it. As a result, resistance is the fuel by which chronic worry spreads. Giving yourself permission to worry sounds, on the surface, like an unwelcome exercise. In the short term and in the long term, you'll see the benefit because (1) you don't have to feel bad resisting it, and (2) you can get your worry out of the way, at least to some degree, so you can get on with your day and your other responsibilities.

If you dedicate a specific future time to worry, the immediate benefit is the ability to postpone worry. Many people find that this enables them to handle large portions of their day relatively clear of worry. However, it only works if you actually do the worry at the time that it is scheduled. If you try to ignore your worries, knowing that you probably won't actually show up for worry time, the postponing probably won't work for you.

So, what I want you to do is whenever you notice that you are full of worry, make a time on a calendar or phone reminder for later that day. Pick a time when you have privacy and don't have to be in an appointment or meeting, have to cook, have to look after the dog or the kids, or have another pressing responsibility. It's usually best to avoid the following times: first thing in the morning upon waking up and last thing you do before going to bed.

Time that I will be worrying is: _____ a.m./p.m.

Now make a list of all the things you are going to worry about during your upcoming worry time so you have an agenda.

1. ________________________________
2. ________________________________
3. ________________________________
4. ________________________________
5. ________________________________
6. ________________________________
7. ________________________________

Come back to this page at that time. Make sure you show up for your worry time. Set a timer for ten minutes and get ready to engage in pure worry. Devote your full attention to worrying and nothing else. Don't engage in other activities, like driving, showering, eating, cleaning, texting, listening to music, riding on a train, and so on. Spend the full ten minutes worrying about whatever items you usually worry about. And don't try to solve problems, reassure yourself, minimize problems, relax, clear your mind, reason with yourself, or take any other steps to stop worrying. Simply worry, which means reciting, repeatedly, lots of "what if" questions about unpleasant possibilities.

Feel free to schedule up to two worry times a day. And lastly, try saying all of these worries out loud, preferably in front of a mirror.

So, how did your first worry time go? Write any reflections below.

People who do this exercise find that it is effective because (1) it externalizes all the junk in their head and gives it air in the light of day and (2) they find worry exhausts itself when they devote all their attention to it. Don't take my word for it. You have to do the time for yourself.

By saying your worries out loud, you are removing the privacy that gives our worries a part of their power. If you chuckled a little while you spoke them out loud, that's common, and also a sign that a worry that feels so true and scary in our mind actually sounds sort of ridiculous. And the other thing is that we often worry endlessly in the background of our lives. This background noise of worry is what helps it gain steam and sneak into all parts of our lives. When you actually turn to give it your full attention, you often find that the power has fizzled out.

When You Don't Feel Like Doing Anything: Avoid Your Avoidance

Oftentimes, we have big projects and responsibilities that we put off or procrastinate on starting because we don't have the energy and sometimes because we secretly fear that we can't actually accomplish the task. Think about a big presentation that you have to prepare. You may not outwardly tell yourself that you are scared to death, but part of you is more nervous than you consciously know. As a result, you avoid the presentation.

In the short term, the avoidance feels good because you don't have to address your anxiety directly. Your avoidance gives you relief. Unfortunately, you delay the inevitable. Eventually, you have to start and finish the exact thing that you have been avoiding except with less time and potentially with less energy and bandwidth. Of course you can continue to distract yourself with easily obtainable pleasures that hijack your productivity. Until you break the cycle, you will continue to avoid important tasks, difficult conversations, and life-changing decisions—all of which are necessary for your psychological fortitude.

The first step is to notice what triggers you to avoid important responsibilities and default to bad habits. If you know what triggers your avoidance, you can create a strategy to overcome it. For example, Anika realized she was watching too much Netflix while an important deadline was sitting unaddressed. If she was being honest, she would acknowledge that she secretly doubted her ability to handle the task. Instead, she told herself that she would indulge in thirty minutes of television, but she failed to set a timer.

Write down a few of the trigger traps (for example feeling incompetent, overwhelmed, tired) that keep you paralyzed.

1. ______________________________

2. ______________________________

3. ______________________________

After listing the traps, think about what you do when you feel like you'd rather avoid doing something.

1. ______________________________

2. ______________________________

3. ______________________________

Now that you are beginning to notice what might trigger you into avoiding doing something and your unhelpful strategies for not being effective, the next step is to take a deep breath. When you start to feel antsy or compelled to act on a bad habit, take a deep breath. Let it out slowly, then take another deep breath. Repeat as necessary. Long, slow breathing calms the brain.

Next, have a go-to activities list. This is a simple list of time-limited things you like to do. Whenever the urge to avoid something comes up and you feel triggered to turn away from the whole day and shut yourself in your house, look back at your handy activity list. Bonus points if things on your activity list are easy, simple, and involve being outside in fresh air or with positive friends or family.

1. ______________________________
2. ______________________________
3. ______________________________
4. ______________________________
5. ______________________________

Next, break down the task you've been avoiding into smaller, more manageable parts. You might begin with planning to work on the task for thirty minutes at a time until it is complete or asking someone with expertise to help.

1. ______________________________
2. ______________________________
3. ______________________________
4. ______________________________
5. ______________________________

When You Have Difficult Thoughts: Challenging Hopelessness

When you are on the way to the airport with only twenty minutes before your flight takes off but stuck in rush-hour traffic, you probably feel pretty frustrated and hopeless. Hopelessness can be linked to depression and is problematic by itself. Though we all get down on ourselves sometimes, you could be someone who has slipped into seeing the world through a lens of hopelessness that important things don't go your way, that you have little control over what will happen to you in the future, and that there isn't much use in trying to pursue your dreams. I am here to tell you that you have options to change your circumstances even if the actions are small. Holding on to the mindset that things can't change will only end as you predict—with no possibility of succeeding, getting help, or finding a solution.

Hopelessness is a myth. Humans are adaptable. While you may have previously adapted poorly to deal with a situation that seemed hopeless, you can switch things up to suit you! We can generate different ideas, make predictions, and move toward positive future opportunities. We can avoid excessive risks and visible dangers. We can solve problems. I understand that we sometimes forget that these capabilities are within reach if we stretch ourselves just a little. Here is an exercise that is similar to the thinking traps exercises from the last chapter. The key is to take time to dispute your hopeless thoughts. Ask your hopelessness a question as a starting point; then answer the question by exploring the options you have at hand. See below for examples.

Hopeless thought: *I don't have what it takes to change.*

Ask it a question: *What can I work at changing that is within my control?*

Answer the question: *I started exercising to work against sad feelings. I've made progress. I can make positive changes. I'm doing that already.*

Now you try.

First hopeless thought: ______________________________

____

Ask it a question: ______________________________

____

Answer the question: ______________________________

____

Second hopeless thought: ______________________________

____

Ask it a question: ______________________________

____

Answer the question: ______________________________

____

Third hopeless thought: ____

____

Ask it a question: ____

____

Answer the question: ____

____

As humans, we find ways to deal with life's adversities the best way that we can. Having a low PF is no different. As a general rule for all of these exercises and skills, recognize your challenge for what it is: a challenge to be overcome when you are ready. Unless you have a hidden superpower, you cannot change the things that happened in the past. Release yourself of the past. You can decide to change today, or you can decide tomorrow. Either way, you are making a decision. If you tell yourself that your fear of something signifies that you are "crazy," then you have put undue pressure on yourself. This pressure will make your situation harder to get out from under. Being crazy is yet another hurdle that you have to overcome—as if you do not have enough to do already. If you instead try to think of your low PF problem as something that is "not helpful," you put yourself on the path to creating solutions that are more likely attainable.

When Racism Impacts Your PF

These days, African American men, women, and children are mistreated and sometimes killed for doing normal things that white people do or could do without a second thought or consequence. In this reality, it is very hard not to feel disgusted, worried, and powerless.

We all witnessed the murder of forty-six-year-old George Floyd as a police officer forced him to the ground, handcuffed him, and kneeled on his neck while he pleaded for help for nearly ten minutes. We have yet to see justice for twenty-six-year-old Breonna Taylor, who was killed when police entered her home while she was asleep in bed. The police weren't supposed to be there and entered the wrong home, but there were no charges for her shooting death. Trayvon Martin walked through a middle-class neighborhood on his way home. He had purchased a bag of Skittles from a nearby store. He did not make it home that night. Instead, he was killed by a neighborhood watchman who had been told to stay in his car and not approach Trayvon. How many times did you watch the video or listen to Diamond Reynolds as she kept her composure while pleading with the police officer, who shot her boyfriend, to tell her that her boyfriend wasn't dead? My own heart broke even more for her daughter who sat still in the back of the car. You never heard the child scream or cry. At some point, she told her mother, "It's okay. I'm right here with you." These stories go on and on because police kill Black people on 300 out of 365 days each year.[7]

There is a sickness in our society that has given you *plenty* of reason to have low PF. When the video of George Floyd's death played over and over in the news, you may have felt keyed up, angry, and at times, sick. As time passed, you may have become emotionally numb to police violence, but when you were subjected to the court trial and the testimony of the bystanders, you relived much of the same intense emotions. Clinically, experts say that your emotional response should be in proportion to the stressful situation. I acknowledge that it isn't so straightforward and not very easy to explain, but while the threats in our society that make you worry are real, there are ways to cope that can be helpful. You can follow these five steps.

Undoing Racism's Negative Effect on Your PF

Step 1. Identify the racial situation that is undermining your PF.

____

____

Step 2. Let it out. In the space below, take time to write down your thoughts and feelings about this situation. Otherwise, the thoughts replay in your mind and can intensify.

____

____

____

____

____

____

____

____

____

Step 3. Identify your pain. In the space below, ask yourself, "What about all of this is most upsetting to me?" Maybe your heart hurts for the murdered young person's mother. Perhaps you wonder if things will ever get better.

____

____

____

____

____

____

____

____

____

____

____

Step 4. Consider your exposure. If the situation you are upset about is in the news, you may have to begin by limiting your exposure to social media, where the outrageous scene plays over and over. Though it is good to be informed, think about what is in your control and how exposure to senseless violence undercuts your PF. Research shows that Black people report poorer emotional health for one to two months following the police shooting of an unarmed Black person.[8]

Social media seems to contribute to vicarious trauma. There is research that shows that African Americans have been experiencing trauma-related anxiety in response to chronic media exposure to violent deaths of African Americans.[9] In any one of these unarmed-shooting incidents, we can imagine someone close to us who could be targeted. Each time you hear of another unnecessary murder of an unarmed person, you feel anger and a sense of helplessness. You may internalize the message that people like you do not matter. You may be saddened or enraged. In any case, these are all reactions to an awful and pervasive problem in our society—a problem that has meaningful psychological consequences.

Step 5. Process the pain with action. Join or start an advocacy group that challenges the use of force in policing or join a larger group, such as Moms Demand Action for Gun Sense in America. This was one step taken by Lucy McBath, the mother of Jordan Davis, who was killed because he was enjoying loud music with his friends. Mrs. McBath is now a United States congresswoman.

The thing about anxiety is that the actual cause of the anxiety does not matter. What matters is what you do in response to your fear and how you manage your worry. The steps laid out in the last two chapters are critical for proactively responding to when your psychological fortitude gets low.

Asking for Help and Getting It When You Need It

There are going to be times that you get to activate your self-care plan and practice responding to your negative thoughts, and yet you still feel your low PF. In times where your PF remains low despite your effort, one the best things to do is also one of the hardest: ask for help.

This can be a scary thing to do. You have to be vulnerable and choose the right person as well as explore (in a precise way) what you need and are asking. This exercise is meant to be an exploration of what you might need and how you can go about getting it. But feel free to share with your confidante so they know they might be called upon in the future.

1. Think of a person you trust fully. This person can be a family member or friend. The key is that you feel safe around them and that you can be honest and vulnerable without feeling judged or attacked. Write their name down and some reason why you might turn to them for help.

2. Think about what you need. What would be most useful for you in this moment? Is it time to decompress? Is it access to mental health care? Is it childcare needs? Try to be as specific as you can about what might restore your PF to a healthier place.

3. Now use the space below to write a script for yourself. Imagine talking to your confidante and what you might say.

4. At this point, you can do a number of things. You can share this script directly with your person in a precautionary way. Or reserve a time in the near future when you can broach it with them. Know that asking for help in this way is neither weak nor selfish. You are doing what you need to feel like you're in better control of your mind, your emotions, and your overall PF. Write what you plan to do.

Keep in mind that many people, even strangers, help one another out all the time. This doesn't have to be a transaction wherein you are required to do something for the other person in exchange for them helping you. If it feels that way, I suggest finding another trusted person. Also, there may be a mental health issue that is beyond the scope of your person to handle. If that's the case, perhaps you two can go over chapter 7 together and enlist their support in helping you get access to professional care.

Wrap Up

Our suffering feels like our norm. It's insane when you think about it. Sadly, anxiety and depression are serious but often hidden problems because you may not know what to look for. Now you have more information.

You probably knew that you have a part of your life that you have to "deal with" and feel you have no choice but to do just that. You suck it up and try to live life. You may even think that this is what it means to have psychological fortitude, but this is where I would have to stop you. If you are constantly managing nagging or intrusive thoughts, have a hard time getting out of bed most days, or avoid social situations because you fear that you will do something to embarrass yourself, you are not living life. Your PF is at 4 at best. If at the end of the day, it feels like a hamster-wheel existence, it is. You may be waiting for something magical to happen, but magical thinking will not solve the problem.

I know it is especially hard to try to get help when you are overwhelmed, your PF is low, and it already takes everything in you to put one foot in front of the other. To add to this, you simply do not have time to take to get help for yourself when you are also responsible for others.

However, when either anxiety or depression goes untreated, it undermines your quality of life. It also undermines aspects of physical health, but especially your ability to maintain or regain health. If you get to a stage of life whereby you have to manage health challenges, know that it is difficult to manage health without high PF.

Since your PF *is* in your control, I advise that you practice maximizing it to the best of your ability before it gets stuck. It can be scary to think about slipping backward, but don't worry, you got this.

CHAPTER 4

Boost Your Readiness for Lifelong Change

I wish you could flip a switch and everything would be all right. The reality is you may be doing great one day, and on the next day, you find yourself feeling defeated and crying in the bathroom or some other secret place. You may even wonder if being overwhelmed is just normal. Everyone is overwhelmed, right?

Real change, unfortunately, cannot happen overnight. Experts in behavioral change suggest change happens over six stages.[10] Yes, six. It is normal to have setbacks, especially when you are not fully ready for change. The change experts that I mentioned would say many who need change often begin in "precontemplation." In this first stage, you don't yet recognize that you can actually make change in your own life. Your frustration isn't much more than a mental exercise. You may not even realize how bad things are.

The second stage, of "contemplation," is when you are recognizing the depth of the problem and starting to think about how life can be better. You may even begin to (prematurely) make change in this phase. However, those changes are unlikely to hold without the third stage, "preparation," which involves developing a specific plan of action.

Once you have mapped out a plan, you can take "actionable steps" in the fourth stage. Action without preparation is a setup. I'll say that again. Action without preparation is a setup. You cannot skip steps if the goal is psychological fortitude that lasts.

Once you've developed a plan and initiated action, you "maintain the plan" in step five by being aware of roadblocks and pitfalls that can set you back. All of these steps together maximize your readiness to boost your PF in a way that can be "sustained over time"—the goal of the sixth step. This overview of the six stages of making a change shows how attempting to boost PF before you are ready can lead to understandable frustration.

When you are ready to go beyond contemplating your life, your efforts will more easily fall into place and you will be much less likely to get sidetracked. When you are sick and tired of your life as it is (and not before), you can commit to practicing self-care and the emergency PF skills you have been developing. I want you to be prepared to fully own that self-care, and I want boosted PF to be your new normal.

You've been tracking your PF rating and found it slowly inching up—maybe even getting to a place where it is the best it's been. That is great news and worth acknowledging and celebrating. If you get sidetracked, you can evaluate: Is there a pre-contemplative part of your mind that says, *I can't take all of this*? Pay attention to any other new roadblocks that come up, become aware of them, and work with them. Along the way, you are fully owning this process for your life.

Once your self-care has a nice rhythm, a next step is to supercharge your PF. Self-care strategies are starting places in your plan. The reality is that they raise the baseline for how you can feel. But they have a cap on just how high they can get your PF. To go further, an attitude change or a perspective shift is what's needed. This is the shift that began with you moving from contemplating whether you are tired of life as it is to planning for change with readiness for action. It is time to shift the priorities within you: emotional wellness needs to be in every aspect of your life.

You might think you are ready, but let's be sure your readiness isn't misdirected. You tell yourself that when things get tough, you *should* woman up and carry on. And you have been willing to keep yourself busy, but that's a part of the problem. It looks so impressive—serving on a time-consuming community board, leading your local Links Inc. chapter, volunteering for the PTA, and being the primary guardian for your elderly aunt as well as your two middle-school-age children, all while showing up as the most well-put-together sista in the room. You do not have the bandwidth to know how you are doing, much less what to do differently. Everything's under control, right? Things will get better once you finish with this one event, or once you figure out how to get out of your current job situation, or once the doctors can give you a proper diagnosis for your aunt's mysterious illness—right?

As a Black woman, I know that we have a tremendous will to hide our pain. What you are going to learn in this chapter is that we all need to shift this willingness to keep on keeping on. We need to put PF at the center of how we see ourselves in the world. We must get intentional about our readiness for change and see mental health as a core part of how we live.

PF Check-In

Before we get intentional about your readiness, let's check in on your PF. Take a few deep breaths. Quiet yourself for a moment. And write down your current psychological fortitude below.

PF rating (0–10): ________

What did you notice about your rating today?

___

___

___

What types of things may be impacting it positively?

___

___

___

What types of things may be impacting it negatively?

___

___

___

What might be keeping your PF higher than it would have been in a similar situation in the past?

___

___

___

Let's add a few more questions to our check-in.

If you've been regularly practicing self-care or using the therapeutic skills from the last chapter, how have you felt about your PF rating?

___

___

___

Is it often higher or lower than you expect?

____

Have you ever felt like your PF rating hasn't quite reflected how you feel?

____

____

____

For you to be able to be honest about your PF rating, you might have to look deeper. We all imagine how we want to be or hear how others want us to be and try to live up to that. But what if that's getting in your way of knowing how you're really doing?

Start Seeing Yourself Anew

Most of us will take major illness—in our ourselves and our loved ones—very seriously. When it comes to our own *mind*, however, we settle for just hoping for the best. It's fascinating and the opposite of what I want to advocate to you in this chapter. Our community often assumes that therapy is for white people. Presumably, pain and suffering are for Black people. I don't know where all we learn this; it seems like it just is.

You get stuck in a paralyzing cycle of struggle—things seem better for a little while, but before you know it, you're back to being overwhelmed. If you don't see examples of true psychological fortitude around you, it can be hard to imagine a different way of being.

To add, you have gotten by thus far without going to therapy and having to tell all of your business, so why start now? You have everything going for you, and everyone around you thinks highly of you. But you know the truth—things are not right. At a minimum, you are not doing as well as you know that you can be doing in your personal life, in your professional life, or in your health. It is time to prioritize your well-being enough to seek a better life for yourself. To do that, you need to see a few things differently—including yourself.

Be willing to let go of who you want people to think you are. Until you do that, you cannot get a good sense of your psychological fortitude. Successful entrepreneur, perfect mom of perfect children, well-connected soror: keeping up personas can send you to an early grave. You certainly cannot reclaim your mind if you can't have a good giggle at your real and sometimes pitiful self.

Part of embracing your readiness for change will involve unpacking the way we think about ourselves. This is good and healthy work to do. But how?

Learn to Say Yes

Jay-Z is arguably one of the most accomplished musical artists and businessmen of his lifetime. In an interview with the executive editor of the *New York Times*, he talked about going to therapy and "growing so much" through the process. At the time of the interview, he was well into his forties. It can take time to get to a place of readiness for growth.

Shonda Rhimes is one of the most shining examples of Black girl magic of the twenty-first century. Her talents are innumerable. Ms. Rhimes showed us how we could be brilliant and emotional and fearless and vulnerable all at the same complicated time. We could do this while still winning and slaying. This was new imagery for a Black woman that we could relate to. Shonda Rhimes did that.

Despite Ms. Rhimes's inspiring success and creativity, she reveals in her book *Year of Yes* that she struggled with severe, debilitating anxiety. This amazing woman declined coveted talk show interviews due to fear. When she was required to attend events, she sometimes sat silently, relying on fellow guests to fill in the silence. She knew her anxiety was a problem, but she was stuck in very early stages of change. She wasn't ready for a different life.

This was Ms. Rhimes's modus operandi until the day her sister made an offhanded comment about the fact that she always said no. Her no's were a shield to manage her anxiety. But one day, her sister inspired her to say yes to everything. Now I don't mean to say you should start skydiving. I think we need to start saying yes to those things our shields used to say *no* to. This is the power of being ready for change, developing a plan, and putting it into action.

When Ms. Rhimes needed encouragement with personal problems, she said yes to close friends and family. She said yes to being vulnerable with people she trusted. She said yes to things that scared her and found out that she was strong enough to overcome them. She said yes to help and yes to alone time when she needed it.

To finally deal with and get past her anxiety, she had to decide to make a change, make herself uncomfortable, and commit even when things got hard, including having a plan for how to deal with hard times. You too can make this decision now that you are ready.

How to Say Yes to You

This is an exercise that seems simple, but the more you do it, the more power it has: the next time that you are in a situation that is a little bit scary—say it's a presentation at work or a difficult conversation with a loved one—say yes to showing up as your whole self.

It's really that simple. And by whole self, I mean the radiant, joyful, intelligent, vulnerable, sometimes emotional person you are. That you. Not the person you feel like you have to be.

Sure, there will be times you are depleted. In those moments, get your PF up with your tried-and-true practices. And get to a place, emotionally, where you can say yes with all of who you are. Let's break it down.

Think of something in the next two weeks that you dread or know will be difficult. But it is important to you. Write it down here:

What kind of thoughts and emotions does thinking about this event bring up for you?

Looking at the previous reflection, what can you tell yourself about why you can still say yes to this? What are all the possible outcomes to this event?

How do you think your best self could show up for this?

Between now and this event, what can you do to ensure you have a high PF going into that difficult situation?

____

____

____

____

And that's it. Our fear of messing up or doing something we are not supposed to often keeps us locked into a life that doesn't feel fulfilling. The truth is that the next step of our PF journey is going to come with some challenges. But it is by getting over those challenges that we enhance our vision of ourselves as someone who does more than simply cope with life's punches. That's the power that saying yes—and the readiness to do so—has for our PF.

Boundaries and When Saying Yes Goes Wrong

There are some times, however, when we say yes to too many things. We find ourselves in charge of too many things because we say yes when we need to say "maybe next time" or simply no. One simple key to distinguishing whether we are saying yes to the right things is to quickly do a PF check-in when considering the activity. If your PF is 5 or lower, you are unlikely to feel good about this yes later on.

As Black women, we need to own how much we take on at the expense of our well-being. Our way of doing things has been an unhealthy form of saying yes too often. In these instances, it can be easy to lose all sense of yourself. This is not what Shonda would do. And not the kind of saying-yes experience that is going to increase your PF.

The reality is that we need to set healthy and appropriate boundaries. A boundary is a dividing line that defines who you are as an individual, how you'll interact with others, and what is outside your capacity. Some boundaries are needed for those who are close to us. Other boundaries are needed for everyone else—individuals we perceive the need to please, perhaps at work, or church, or in the community.

Some boundaries define what's *me* (my body, my feelings, my property, my responsibilities, and so forth) and what's *not me*. Boundaries also communicate how we want to be treated by others, what's okay and what's not okay with us, and how close we want to get (physically and emotionally) to others.

When you set boundaries, you assert your individuality. We all have our own thoughts, feelings, values, goals, and interests. But sometimes others are threatened or confused by our differences and want us to think, feel, "be there," and act as they do. We, too, may be afraid of being different, assuming it will lead to criticism or rejection, and go along with situations we don't want to be in, allowing others to tell us who we are and what we need to do.

Psychologists sometimes use the term "enmeshment" to describe this. In enmeshed relationships, there aren't boundaries. Everyone is expected to toe the line, meaning everyone should think, feel, and behave the same. In an enmeshed or boundaryless relationship, you live your life based on what other people want you to do or what they think is right instead of deciding for yourself.

Boundaries create a healthy separation between you and others and define who you are, so you can be yourself and make choices that are right for you. Or, as Prentis Hemphill once described, boundaries are the distance at which I can love you and me simultaneously.

You might avoid setting boundaries because you're afraid that boundaries will damage your relationships by creating distance or conflict. Maybe you fear that you won't be perceived as a team player especially when others fail to establish boundaries. It's true, setting your boundaries may initially be met with some resistance and even retaliation from other people. Still most people will adjust to your boundaries, and your relationships will be strengthened by clearer communication, fewer misunderstandings and conflicts, and greater trust, respect, and connection. You will have peace of mind that you prioritized saying yes to you. I want you to be ready to set boundaries just for you.

Your boundaries must meet your unique needs. So I can't simply give you a list of generic boundaries and expect they will meet your needs. This is why the first step to setting boundaries is to clarify what you need and want. Do this by asking yourself four questions:

1. What boundary-related problems am I experiencing?
2. What are my unmet needs?
3. How do I feel?
4. What outcome do I want? What do I want to accomplish with my boundaries?

So let's try an exercise to practice setting a healthy boundary.

What boundary problem am I experiencing? Does anyone ask something of me that I would rather say no to, but I keep saying yes?

____

____

____

When you experience boundary-related problems, like the one you wrote about above, there's an underlying unmet need, something that you need but aren't getting or that is being asked of you but that you don't want to give. It is causing you distress or discomfort of some kind. Identifying these unmet needs will also give you valuable information about what boundaries to set so these needs do get met.

Using the same boundary-related problem, identify your unmet needs. Here are a couple examples:

Problem: *Tanya is consistently late.*

Unmet need(s): *Respect.*

Problem: My *job asking me about work while I'm on vacation.*

Unmet need(s): *Value and respect.*

Problem: ____

Unmet need(s): ____

There are countless reasons for our feelings, and boundary violations aren't always what's behind them. But even if you discover that your feelings aren't pointing you toward a boundary issue, paying more attention to your feelings and being aware of what they're telling you always helps and never hinders.

In particular, pay attention to the following feelings, as they're common emotional responses to boundary violations.

Angry
Resentful
Frustrated
Annoyed
Irritated
Pissed
Mad
Furious
Livid
Outraged
Bothered

Afraid
Scared
Terrified
Worried
Distressed

Hurt
Sad
Depressed
Hopeless
Miserable
Upset
Unimportant

Uncomfortable
Uneasy
Awkward
Tense
On edge
Embarrassed
Ashamed

Put words to how you felt when you experienced the boundary-related problem that you've identified.

For example:

Problem: *Tanya is consistently late.*

Feeling(s): *Annoyed, disrespected, unimportant.*

Problem: *My job is asking me about work while I'm on vacation.*

Feeling(s): *Frustrated, tense, miserable.*

Problem: ______________________________

Feeling(s): ______________________________

Once you've identified the problem, your unmet needs, and your feelings, you can put them together to create a clear statement about the outcome you want when you set this boundary. I've found that using this specific formula is the most effective way to clarify what you truly need and want.

I need ______________ (need) and want to feel ______________ (feeling) when ______________________________ (situation) happens.

You'll notice that we aren't focusing on how to achieve this yet, only on what you need and how you want to feel.

Now, incorporate the problems, needs, and feelings you've already identified into this formula to create your desired outcome statement. Use the formula above if it's helpful. Tip: The way you want to feel is usually the opposite of how you feel when this problem occurs.

____

____

____

____

____

____

Implement Your Boundaries

Use the following questions to plan how and when you'll implement your new boundaries. Some of the action items in your plan may be difficult or unpleasant, and you might consciously or unconsciously avoid them. Creating a specific plan and timeline will help you be accountable and increase the likelihood of carrying out your plan.

What will you do to set this boundary? Describe the actions that you'll take and the words that you'll use to communicate your boundary to others. Be as specific as possible.

Example: *If Tanya invites me to get together when I have limited time or to go to an activity with a fixed start time, I'll say, "Unfortunately, that day (or activity) doesn't work for me. How about getting together on ____________ (alternate date) to do ____________ (alternate activity) instead?"*

In the other example: *If I get an email from my supervisor while on vacation, I'll say, "I am not in a position to help with this at this time, but I will prioritize it when I return on ____________ (alternate date)."*

Your new boundary:

____

____

____

____

____

____

____

When will you do this? (Include date and time, if possible.)

____

____

What action or change, if any, do you need to request from someone else? Tip: Don't make your requests just yet. You'll want to read chapter 5 and use the strategies discussed when you make your requests.

____

____

____

____

____

When will you make this request?

____

____

The key to a good boundary is to (a) be willing to do this for yourself and (b) remain encouraged. Boundary setting is a lifelong journey that ebbs and flows. You will get better at it the more you practice. But boundaries, by definition, move and change shape. Go easy on yourself and know that we all struggle to do this well. But like saying yes, the real skill is to stay willing to do it when it is required.

Be Ready and Willing to Grow

For some people the ability to say yes to things that scare them or set boundaries for themselves and say no to other people's requests comes easy. They are willing, almost by nature, to protect themselves from being imposed on by others. They do this even if the other person will criticize them. Some of us don't have that mindset. We might find ourselves thinking before we even start, *This won't go well*, or *I'm just not good at this*. If this sounds like something you think, then congratulations, you might have a mindset issue.

A mindset is attitude or perspective about how the world works and your own capabilities within it. Researchers have identified two distinct mindsets: a fixed mindset is one where you feel that you are who you are and that you have a certain amount of finite ability, and a growth mindset is one where you feel like you are adaptable and can learn and develop a new ability.[11]

Regardless of actual abilities, the two mindsets have astounding effects on achieving your work, social, and personal goals and living a life that you value.

Fixed mindset: The belief that you have a certain amount of an ability or skills—perhaps high, perhaps low—and little that you can do to change this. With the fixed mindset, you:

- avoid challenges—choose safe or easy tasks
- run from setbacks
- hide and worry about mistakes
- avoid asking for help from others because their efforts just don't meet your standards (lest they seem to have deficiencies).

Growth mindset: The belief that although you may start with a particular level of ability or attribute, you can develop your skill or attribute. With a growth mindset, you:

- take on more challenges
- are more resilient in the face of difficulty
- adapt and learn from mistakes
- recruit other people as mentors or resources.

With a fixed mindset, the goal is to figure out whether you are adequate. In life, there are two sets of people that you will have feedback from: adoring fans and harsh critics. Both sets can spark thoughts of judgment and ignite a fixed mindset. Whether you receive praise or blame, the result can be aggressive comparisons with others, dismissal of your important efforts, and heightened focus on measuring how good you are. It can deflect you from your growth goal. How do you recast adoration and harsh criticism into clear and specific directions for feeling better? Research has continually found that you are not born with either mindset but develop one as you get older. Even better, you can shift from one to the other.

In the case of adapting an attitude of willingness about putting your mental health first, it is important to find a growth mindset for yourself because it will give you the momentum you need to keep your PF high.

Be Your Own Growth-Mindset Coach

In the following exercise, you will become the encouraging and strategic coach when you hear yourself (or others) passionately praise or severely criticize you. This is the coach that gets you back on the path toward your growth goal when your performance outstrips or falls short. This is the coach who attends to your development, does an analysis, and forges an explicit plan to build on the positive and brave the negatives.

Write down all the harsh-critic thoughts on the left, and on the right, respond as would a helpful, realistic coach, acknowledging strengths and weakness with a specific plan to tackle the weaknesses.

An example with harsh self-talk: A single, working mother forgets that she has a scheduled parent-teacher conference for her eight-year-old son, Malcolm. She had hoped to get some insight into some of her son's difficulty with reading assignments. Her heart sinks, she feels angry at herself when she realizes that she missed her appointment, and then she launches into severely critical self-talk.

Below is her growth-mindset coach worksheet.

Harsh Critic	Growth-Mindset Coach
What an idiot I am! *If I had an ounce of brains, I wouldn't have missed this conference.* *So embarrassing—this shouldn't have happened.* *I'm not organized enough.* *Malcolm's teacher will think I'm a bad mother.*	*Upsetting that I missed the conference.* *How did that happen? I have a lot going on with my job and didn't check my personal calendar this morning. Maybe I could get into the habit of checking my personal calendar when I have my morning coffee. This doesn't mean I'm a bad mother. I really care about Malcolm's progress. I will reach out to his teacher, apologize, and see if I can reschedule in person or by phone.*

Note the difference between the harsh-critic self-talk and the growth-mindset coach responses. How would the harsh critical voice impact motivation? Do you see that the helpful coach acknowledges the problem?

Now you try.

Write about a difficult situation you've had recently or something that didn't go as you hoped:

Next, write the comments you'd hear from a critic in the left column. In the right column, try to imagine a strategy for the same situation that you, as your own growth-mindset coach, would implement.

Harsh Critic	Growth-Mindset Coach

The real key here with having a growth mindset is staying in contact with your willingness to work on yourself, in feeling as if you can adapt, change, and get better. That is what I imagine Shonda Rhimes finally felt when she began saying yes to things. And it is what you are going to continue to do on your path to maintaining high PF.

Wrap Up

Every single person on earth needs reinforcements and a plan of action to be successful and to maintain a reasonably healthy lifestyle. That's what this chapter has been all about. Your readiness for meaningful change is tricky because it isn't a quick pill to swallow or a specific habit to create. It is about the intention you bring to yourself and to your life.

The message I want you to get from this chapter is you have to set yourself up to reclaim your mind. It has to be a central part of how you consider living. You cannot achieve real life change until you are sick and tired of the way things are and ready to commit to your self-care. You need to be ready and willing to bravely say yes to something that is challenging or that impacts you negatively in the short term. The payoff is that you can live with less stress and more joy. And you need to be willing to set healthy and positive boundaries so you are not stretched thin or abused by other people's demands on your time.

And lastly, when things get really tough, your willingness is crucial in asking for and getting help. Most of what we've covered in this chapter is self-driven. But there are times when you can't go it alone, and being willing, especially, to ask for help can help you tremendously. Whether you are a CEO of a major corporation, a stay-at-home mom of three, or a graduate student anticipating your first "real job," you need backup from time to time. I am here to tell you that you do not have to wait until things get worse. You can do something right now to call in reinforcements. This is what you do in the name of your psychological fortitude.

CHAPTER 5

Strengthen Your Resilience to Overcome Racism and Stigma

Too often, your PF is stifled by everyday racism. At times, things seem to be going from bad to worse. Crises rotate from police violence to racist supervisors on the job, to being kicked out of a coffee shop for doing the same thing as white people, and then back to police violence.

All the things you have done thus far in this book have been about increasing your well-being and learning to reclaim your mind despite it all. It has been a personal journey of developing new skills, habits, and a mindset that can set you on the path of full-time emotional wellness. On their own, the tips in this book work great. If you never have to go to work, or drive around town, or interact with "sometimey" people in the world, I can almost guarantee you will have a high PF.

The problem is that is not realistic. We have to put ourselves out into the world. And one of the biggest issues for your PF, no matter how expert you are at minding your self-care and affirming your Black identity, is that racism can be relentless. Too many segments of this world have been designed to degrade your mind and make you feel worse about yourself for reasons you do not control.

So if you are going to keep progressing and truly take back your mind, you have to address any racism you may have unintentionally internalized and find a way to stay resilient in the face of an unkind, unequal, and unjust society.

PF Rating Check-In

Before we start this part of our self-care journey, let's check in on your PF. Take a few deep breaths. Quiet yourself for a moment. Write down your current psychological fortitude rating below.

PF rating (0–10): ________

What did you notice about your rating today?

____

____

____

What types of things may be impacting it negatively?

____

____

____

What types of things might be keeping your PF higher than it would have been in a similar situation in the past?

____

____

____

How Racism Impacts Your PF

You have likely experienced racism and microaggressions at many points in your life. You know what it is when you see it. Scientists can say with confidence that racism is bad for Black mental health.[12] This is an area where numerous studies converge on this one conclusion. Multiple experts using different approaches for studying racism-related problems have determined that racial discrimination is psychologically and physically harmful to Black people.[13]

In a study of Black women in Detroit, Michigan, researchers collected data for 343 women over the course of five years. In this study, they found that more discrimination was associated with poorer health and more depression.[14] This was true even after considering the age, income level, and education of the study participants. Typically, older people and those with less formal education and fewer resources tend to have poorer physical health, but that simply did not matter in the Detroit study. One preliminary study found that atherosclerosis, which is typically associated with smoking and high cholesterol, was linked to discrimination experiences among African American women.[15] Again, the researchers controlled for other factors that commonly lead to atherosclerosis. Racism was bad, and neither age nor social status mattered.

Explore Racism's Impacts on You

Racial microaggressions have very personal effects. They can stimulate self-doubt and secret beliefs such as *I only got this opportunity because I'm Black*. It's important to take an honest look at any of your beliefs about race. Respond to the following questions to explore more of your personal experiences.

Think back to a time when you heard or experienced a racial microaggression—something that would qualify as subtle disrespect for a person of color. Write it here, and then identify the theme and embedded message.

Now think about the tone of that experience and its theme and describe them here.

And what do you think the message of that comment or that experience was for you?

What were your thoughts, feelings, and behaviors *during* this racial microaggression—in the moments you were experiencing it?

What I thought:

What I felt:

What I did:

____

____

____

____

____

What were the effects of the experience? What message did it convey to you about yourself or other people? How long did it continue to affect your emotions, thoughts, and experiences?

____

____

____

____

Take a moment to explore these nine racial microaggression categories you may experience most frequently.[16] Rank each item in this list from 1 (most frequent) to 9 (least frequent).

____ Alien in one's own land: "You don't belong."

____ Intelligence branding: "Black people aren't as smart as white people."

____ Color blindness: "I don't see you as Black."

____ Assumptions of criminality: "You're probably going to steal something."

____ Denial of individual racism: "All kinds of people experience discrimination."

____ Myth of meritocracy: "Anyone can be successful with hard work."

____ Diminishing cultural values and communication styles: "Black people are ghetto."

____ Second-class citizen: For example, being ignored while shopping or waiting for a service.

____ Environmental microaggressions. For example, seeing magazine or other ads that have no Black people or people of color.

What did you notice about your rankings of racial microaggressions? As you look at the most frequent ones you experience, what are the feelings associated with the ones that are most frequent or least frequent? Are feelings of anger, self-doubt, shame, guilt, fear, sadness, or other emotions associated more or less with some of the categories on the list?

____

____

____

____

____

____

____

____

____

____

The best way to minimize the harm of experiencing racism is to notice what's happening as soon as possible and be able to interrupt and respond by setting a boundary as we practiced in the last chapter. You can do this through your internal dialogue (*That is this person's problem and doesn't reflect on me; I'm sick and tired of this disrespect; I need to connect with someone who understands my frustration*) or external dialogue ("You are wrong, and what you said was disrespectful"). You do need to acknowledge and validate the feelings that come up for you too. If you experience anger, you may need to breathe through that anger before you channel it into setting a boundary. If you experience fear, you may need to take care of yourself and digest what has happened before you set a boundary.

When I talk about responses to microaggressions, I use the categories of internal and external dialogue for a few reasons. Sometimes racial microaggressions are happening within a context that feels unsafe—like in a predominantly white environment, or while you are traveling outside your home, or even during a job evaluation for promotion—when you could face repercussions for speaking out. So it might not always be safe to externalize your thoughts to the person committing the microaggression. But it is always important to be on top of your game with your internal dialogue, like we did in chapter 2. Negative self-talk is not going to help you. Instead, it will allow the situation to negatively affect your PF as you internalize the racist messages you just received.

Internalized Oppression: When Racism Gets Inside Your Thoughts

Before we dive into ways to immerse yourself in cultural traditions that affirm your Blackness, I want to address how much you are immersed in a reality that does the opposite and sets your psychological fortitude back.

I know that mainstream society has tried to convince you that we are all the same and that Black people who "make everything about race" are the real problem. This is an opinion (and not an informed one). I know that it can be intimidating to examine and rethink your current reality. You've probably had some clues that you were operating in an alternate reality, perhaps even a fake reality, but could not quite put your finger on the "it" that drove this underlying suspicion. The "it" is that your ancestors had to hide who they were in order to survive. By hiding their true African self over generations, you inherited the story that you are just American or that being African American is just about your skin color. One profound quote that has been attributed to James Baldwin asserts, "To be African American is to be African with no memory and to be American with no privilege."

Many of us are aware that we lack white privileges, but very few of us are aware of how we have unintentionally adopted Eurocentric beliefs about Black people. Take a moment to get real. Only you need to know this, so be honest with yourself. Then, answer these questions.

On a scale from 0 to 100, with 100 meaning that you absolutely believe the statement, rate how much you believe the following statements.

____ Black people are inherently not as smart as white people.

____ Black people who have light skin and eyes are more attractive than Black people who have darker skin and eyes.

____ Black people are inherently more criminal than white people.

This is a crude approach, but if your rating falls in the range of 50 to 100 on any one of these statements, you will benefit from reeducating yourself. You have internalized some notion that white people are superior to Black people, so you have made—and will continue to make—decisions based on this belief. The truth you need to discover for yourself is that Black people may do things differently, but this is a difference and not a deficiency. The characteristics that make us different are rooted in something deeply creative and unique and spiritual. We do not have to be limited by others' imaginations.

If you add your three scores and divide by three to achieve a crude racism self-assessment score that is 15 to 49, you will still benefit from some reorientation. Mainstream society is constantly reinforcing that racial differences are due to the inferiority of Black people. It is almost everywhere we look, from the challenges that have arisen in the Black community due in large part to attempts to overcome systemic racism, to the health care system that creates severe mistrust in us, to the injustice system with its many layers that cause problems for Black people who try to peacefully live life. These challenges will take time to overcome, even within yourself. So I strongly encourage you to recognize your internalized racism and how it impacts your thinking and behavior on an ongoing basis. And always seek new ways to bolster who you are as an African-descended person.

Examine and Reimagine Racialized Thinking

In this healing practice, you will examine what's called your "racial socialization" (basically how we come to understand our Blackness from the culture around us) and identify the messages you *needed to hear* to have a more holistic, truthful, and helpful racial socialization.[17] Let's first start with reflecting on how your life was as you were growing up.

When you were born, racial stereotypes were already laid out in the world. Those who raised you did their best to prepare you for an unwelcoming society. Write about the racial messaging your family passed on to you—messaging such as, "You will have to work twice as hard (as white people) to get half as far," or that otherwise alerted you to an unfair world.

____

____

____

____

You likely picked up on "rules" about being Black that were unwritten and unspoken. If your family attended Black churches or socialized with Black people to the exclusion of others, that behavior may have shaped your expectations about acceptable interactions outside your family. As you think back, what unspoken messages did you learn?

____

____

____

____

____

As you think about the world outside your family and close community, what messages did you learn about being Black or African American? Were there rules about trusting doctors, police, and even banks or banking establishments? What rules did you learn as you think about this now?

These rules have likely benefitted and protected you in some ways. That is, at least in part, why they have been passed down from generation to generation—they have helped your ancestors *and you* to survive systems of oppression. What are some ways that you have benefitted from the rules you learned early in life and into adulthood?

It is time to revisit what you learned about being Black as you were growing up. While the messages were helpful for that time in your life, they may need revising, especially if they led to any self-limiting beliefs you may have now.

Consider messages that could have benefitted you but that you did not receive. What are some messages that you needed to hear to be a more psychologically "complete" individual?

Write down messages or examples that you needed from family, family friends, neighbors, and teachers about who you were as an African American or Black child or teenager.

Identify three main messages you learned from your earlier racial socialization that you would like to change right now. For instance, a younger you might write down that you learned your race was something you could affirm and embrace only in certain environments and not something you take pride in everywhere. Write your early racial socialization messages here. Use the additional lines if you want to write more than three.

1. ____

____

____

2. ____

____

____

____

3. ____

____

____

____

4. ____

____

____

____

5. ____

____

____

____

Next, identify three ways you can shift these earlier racial socialization messages; basically, identify ways you can take a stand, reframe racial stereotypes and belief patterns, and interrupt patterns in your thinking, feelings, and behaviors that limit how you see yourself as a grown adult. You might write how you can correct any internalized negative messages about being Black so you can consider new career opportunities, travel more broadly, and embrace who you are, unapologetically. Again, there are a few extra lines in case you feel that you are on a roll right now and want to identify more.

1. ______________________________

____

____

2. ______________________________

____

____

____

3. ______________________________

____

____

____

4. ______________________________

____

____

____

5. ______________________________

____

____

____

Write out what you think your life would be like now if you heard different types of messages or learned from different examples of what it means to be Black in the US. Include messages you needed to receive to hold on to your humanity and healing from racism.

How did it feel to reflect on (1) what your mindset might have been if it had been allowed to evolve in a world free from racism and (2) steps you could take toward that outcome? Did you feel excited, hopeful, or motivated, or sad, lost, angry, or worried? Remember that all of these feelings are normal. Interrogating racism requires raising your awareness and knowledge about what it actually is and how it works, not only in the world, but also in your own life.

As you make decisions to change, like in the last part of the previous exercise, and learn new skills to achieve that change, you can feel exhausted and overwhelmed. It may seem like you'll never be able to "fix" the racism in the world or in your life. But I promise you this: doing the work of healing and reclaiming your mind is better than doing nothing.

Wakanda Is the Antidote

When was the last time that you saw yourself and people who looked like you tapping into their brilliance without having to bend to what was acceptable and white-washed? As you may have noticed from our last exercise, the manner in which we see ourselves directly impacts our mood, thinking, self-esteem, aspirational goals, and vision. That's why I conjure up the fictional land of Wakanda.

Whether or not you saw the groundbreaking movie *Black Panther*, you likely witnessed our community's excitement for the release of that film. We wore coordinating African attire and put on our own social media productions. I, too, went out and got a new 'fit for the occasion. But our clothing wasn't the whole story. "Wakanda forever" became a unifying new mantra for people of African descent around the world. We know what it means when we say, "Wakanda forever!" with pride and enthusiasm. *Black Panther* was everything, and there is a reason why.

If you saw the film, it may have transported you to a place that spoke to your soul. Beautiful, heroic, creative, loyal people were on full display. We saw ourselves in the most positive and perhaps even (for some) unimaginable light. In the movie, women were not subordinate. They were brilliant. They were in charge. It was an amusing highlight of the movie when the young sister so naturally referred to "the colonizer." In Wakanda, Black people were in charge of everything, including what the world knew about them. They knew who they were. At times, they were uncompromising so they could ensure their survival.

If you feel you are drowning in any of the psychological problems I have described in these past chapters, it is high time you connect to a source of psychological fortitude that can get you through. Connecting with who you are, genuinely (not limited by myths of the "dark continent"), can help you recover the resourcefulness you need to build a life worth living and passing on to future generations.

There is an African proverb that says, "No matter how long a log stays in the water, it doesn't become a crocodile." To me, that means no matter how much of your identity has been robbed or how many generations your ancestors were held captive in North America, you will always be African.

Black psychologists have conducted numerous studies that show that when Black men, women, and children have a positive sense of who we are as Black people, we thrive in quality of life and overall well-being. There seems to be an undeniable connection between being in touch with your Blackness, and specifically your Africanness, and your psychological fortitude. My research shows that African Americans who do not see their Black selves in a positive way are at an increased risk for suicide.[18] On the other hand, a positive connection to Black identity protects us to some degree through psychological "buffers." When you have a buffer, bad things can happen, but they do not have as much of a negative effect on you compared to someone who does not have a buffer. This Black resilience has the power to boost your PF and keep it high even in the face of daily traumas like racism.

This next series of exercises are meant to help you prioritize your psychological fortitude by intentionally connecting with your authentic identity. This connection can reinforce your own well-being in addition to providing strategies for passing resilience on to the next generation. I invite you to explore what being Black means to you.

Reclaim Our History

Dr. Asa Hilliard hit the mark when he pointed out that our lack of historical knowledge disables us. We must begin to challenge what we think we know about ourselves. This is why an important step in your rehabilitation is to read the truth about yourself in texts that expose you to both historical and contemporary narratives. Here are some topics to explore. I recommend that you search them online now to get enough of a sense of them to reflect on your own experience. Then read the suggested resources to learn more.

1. Read about what the (Black) Moors contributed to European civilization. Their advances in many aspects of civilization lifted Europe out of the Dark Ages and heralded the Renaissance. Write down the ways this history touches you most. How is this meaningful to you? If you weren't familiar with their contributions, how do you feel as you read about them now?

2. We are not taught in most schools that all of humanity descended from an African woman. Reflect on what knowing this does for your self-esteem and would do for your daughter's sense of who she is as a young Black woman—as an African woman.

Then read Cheikh Anta Diop's *The African Origin of Civilization: Myth or Reality.* Take notes about your feelings in a journal as you do. You can also share your insights with a close friend or family member.

3. Begin to understand how Black people came to be so systematically lost through indoctrinating schools. Take some time to reflect on the impact generations of missing information and incomplete education has had on you and your family. This is how you begin to undo messaging that has undermined psychological, economic, educational, and political progress.

____

____

____

____

____

Read Carter G. Woodson's *Mis-Education of the Negro* to learn more.

4. Reflect on how oppression has infiltrated our minds. Write down examples of the ways you think and your children think as a result. What are the ways you observe oppression happening in your own thoughts? Do you second-guess your talents and abilities? Do you second-guess that you deserve a better life? Do you second-guess that you deserve and can have joy?

____

____

____

____

____

After contemplating your experience, read Dr. Na'im Akbar's *Breaking the Chains of Psychological Slavery* to begin to find inner freedom.

Now let's further explore how this history can impact you. Think of something you learned recently about Black history or culture. It doesn't have to be ancient history, but a recent story in

Black culture that resonates with you. For example, I recently read a piece on the Maroon settlements in Virginia's Great Dismal Swamp. These villages of Black folks survived for generations in a tough environment away from the white gaze and chattel slavery that surrounded them on all sides. This story reconnected me to our history of resilience and adaptability.

Choose a historical story or perhaps a contemporary story of someone having overcome racial injustice—a story that challenged how you thought about yourself and your obligation to help create change. Write it down.

What thoughts do you have when you reflect on this story?

How does it make you feel?

What does this inspire you to learn more about?

I encourage you to pause and be with yourself whenever you encounter stories like this—and to seek out more of them. Be determined in your curiosity because we have a lot of history that has been denied or rewritten for hundreds of years. So much happened that is worth knowing. History shares who we were so we can know more about who we are now. Learn about who we are, and about yourself, by embracing powerful new insights and perspectives that Black scholars and thinkers are offering now and resurrecting those that have been buried for years. The inspiration that you feel when you read historical narratives is exactly what you need to increase your psychological fortitude, especially when you're feeling tired and unmotivated. These perspectives resonate because they fill an emptiness deep in your soul. Take your time, but absorb all that you can.

While you're out claiming things, you might as well reclaim your hair and your language. Two things that we find ourselves referring to as "bad" are "bad hair" and "bad English."

Reclaim Our Hair

In recent years, tremendous positive energy has shifted toward valuing our natural hair. You might argue that blond hair and light-colored contacts are not about any kind of self-hate. Instead, you thought the lighter eyes were pretty. You may even describe naturally kinky hair as "bad" hair. This is one of those things that you will have to expand your thinking on. The only *good* hair is the hair that is growing healthily out of your head. You may be especially vulnerable if you work in a corporate setting or even in media where you would be frowned upon if you wear your natural hair. At minimum, you anticipate uncomfortable comments or quiet stares. In too many instances, the comments will happen. In other stances, no one says anything about your hair, but this is what you have told yourself as a consequence of internalized racism. If you struggle with your natural hair, let's expand how you see your natural beauty.

What have you told yourself about your hair recently?

____

____

____

____

____

What might you tell yourself when you remove your fears of how others could react to seeing your natural hair?

If you've been critical of your natural hair in the past, what can you tell yourself now?

If you do not have a favorite hairstylist, research one who specializes in healthy hair or natural hair. What new style can you explore the next time you have an appointment with the hairstylist?

Describe what Black beauty looks like to you. As you do, notice if a sense of authenticity and power come to mind.

As you claim the beauty and style that makes sense to you, make sure your claim is rooted in whatever is most true and most authentic for you. Give yourself permission to boost your PF inside by connecting with your uniquely beautiful self on the outside.

Reclaim Our Language

Our natural hair is not the only way that we malign our natural way of being. Part of Black culture is how we talk. Unfortunately, we have labeled much of our speech as "bad English." Putting our culture down for surviving will compromise your authenticity and your well-being. Code-switching, when you shift from your more comfortable African American Vernacular to Standard American English, is understandable. However, rejecting Black English as ghetto or slang is problematic. A lot of what we call slang is African American Vernacular, but very few of us know the difference. Like you, I was conditioned to how we are "supposed" to talk to keep from "sounding ignorant." Even if it was a legitimate vernacular, I learned to avoid much of it depending on who the audience was.

Write down messages you heard when you were young about the way you spoke.

How did these messages make you feel?

Reflect on what you *believed* about Black speech.

Can you see how you may have been brainwashed to buy into African inferiority? Meanwhile, Black people are out here surviving brilliantly. How we talk is part of who we are! 50 Cent with no S. That's African. The missing G's—that's African. It is not lazy talk. Most of us use African American Vernacular English (AAVE). Of course we use slang, but AAVE is not slang or lazy. Even if she "ain't never" on time, it's not bad English. It is governed by a West African grammar structure and English words for a people who were self-taught in horrid conditions and were segregated far longer than integrated.

Do you know the origins of how you speak? What stories or legacies or geographies are reflected in your words?

____

____

____

Reflect on how those origins can be a source of pride. What does how you speak say about the legacy you carry and your gifts?

____

____

____

____

____

____

____

____

Consider this, and then read Geneva Smitherman's *Talkin and Testifyin*. In your day-to-day interactions, notice language more. Perhaps you can see Black English as something genuine, as part of who we are, and therefore something to celebrate. Even more, it is to be applauded. Imagine how creative and intelligent you have to be to create language!

Reclaim Black Culture Beyond "American"

You already know that your spirituality is a huge part of your culture. Lord knows that you would not have survived this long with your mind partly intact if you did not have a strong sense of faith in God, passed down over many generations. This is the thing about culture—we learn who we are from the previous generation. In the same way, if you pass on to your children that they are "just American," they lose their true identity. You must intentionally label that which is "African" to allow yourself positive messages about who you are. Let's explore your sense of culture.

What is American culture to you? List five things that come to mind when you think of it.

1. ________________________________
2. ________________________________
3. ________________________________
4. ________________________________
5. ________________________________

What is African culture to you? List five things that come to mind when you think of it.

1. ________________________________
2. ________________________________
3. ________________________________
4. ________________________________
5. ________________________________

Black culture is African in origin. If you recoil from this truth or if you are uncomfortable with your connection to the African continent, you would greatly benefit from a reintroduction to the Motherland. Do not filter knowledge through the racist American lens that would have us willingly separate ourselves from the ingenuity and depth of creativity that being African holds for us. So I will say again, Black culture is African because your ancestors brought their culture from various places, mostly West Africa. They did not bring their culture from Europe. African culture is distinct, and it was preserved in ways you do not know because our habits were called "backwards" though our ancestors accessed culture to survive the best way they knew how. We adapted to our circumstances, but the foundation is African.

You might think Black history began in 1619, with the transatlantic slave trade, but you need to look much farther back to the origins of humanity to understand your African identity. Write three things you have heard about the people, history, or resources on the African continent that made you curious to know more.

____

____

____

Go beyond your own stereotypes about life on the continent to achieve an unbiased perspective. Since it's a continent with unimaginable cultural diversity, you'll need to home in on countries that you're interested in learning more about, maybe as a result of a DNA test or a past PBS episode of "Finding Your Roots" with Dr. Henry Louis Gates. Write down the countries, geographical areas, or specific ethnic groups that you want to focus on learning about.

____

____

____

Turn to the African studies department of a university you're associated with or is local to you. Explore their website and follow links to videos and recommended readings. Also, involve your children by reading children's books with them. Stories that are dedicated to them are more likely to resonate with them. Look into stories of Anansi the Spider for popular West African folktales. Explore the books that are featured by Africa Access: http://africaaccessreview.org. There are so many ways to approach your African cultural identity. It all starts with nurturing your curiosity.

Reclaim Your Ancestors' Stories

If your family participates in family reunions, use those occasions to talk to older family members about what your family was like before you were born. Older family members are living history. Perhaps you have already done this or have relatives who love telling family stories. Write down what you have learned from them.

What was life like for them growing up?

What kinds of things did people do for one another that they miss in their neighborhood now?

Are there any family stories that they hold? Summarize a few here. Then go buy a journal to devote to these stories and write down everything you've heard. Oral histories are important and treasured, but the act of writing often inspires you to dig deeper.

This one may be challenging as families often recall hard times and pain more readily, but what memories give them the most pride?

Based on what you have gathered from family stories, let's create one of your own. Imagine you have an ancestor who lived so long ago that no one alive in your family can trace your roots to her—they only have stories. I'll soon invite you to do this yourself, but first consider how I did it.

In Ghana, this ancestor was Ada, which means "first daughter." Our ancestors were very intentional about naming traditions. Names had meaning often linked to the infant's spirit, the situation surrounding the infant's birth, or perhaps the day of the week. In West Africa, we had names that had meaning. Perhaps your parents gave you a name that would allow you to fit in, but you gave your daughter an African name that has meaning, like Nia or Asha.

In Ghana, an ancestral grandmother Ada lived in a community with her sisters and their children and families. Some of her sisters were actually cousins, but there was no language or distinction for "cousins." They were sisters and brothers. Everyone looked out for one another.

Individuals survived because they were part of a community that worked together. They got what was needed from the nearby land. They had chores and responsibilities, but no one was in a hurry when they spent time talking about the day or who fell out of a tree while picking fruit. Time wasn't about the clock, but it was about being present for a neighbor or honoring God and those who had passed on. The distant future did not matter as much as the present. No place was more important than where they were. The importance of family, Ada's protectiveness of her play-cousins who weren't even blood relatives, protecting traditions, and her strong connection to a Higher Power—these are part of a cultural heritage that was passed on.

Now you try. Take a few deep breaths and imagine your ancestor. Your version of Ada. Picture her in your mind. What is her name?

Where on the African continent is she?

What are the details of her life?

What wisdom does she have to share with you?

Now take a moment to feel gratitude. What would you want to say to your ancestor if you could talk to her today?

____

____

____

____

____

What traditions and family stories would you want to pass on to your future generations?

____

____

____

____

____

Reclaim Our Joy, Together

To be educated in a way that matters, you must accept that the way people communicate and their profound sense of creativity, style, and spirituality are no accident. Reclaiming your mind is planning potlucks with other families and also about forming book clubs to read books by Black authors that center on Black experiences. Share stories about the origins of traditional African food that shows up on contemporary family menus. Research jazz and blues music and how they influenced some of the music of today.

Consider each story you encounter. It's not just a fictional narrative, but a representation of a culture from which you have been disconnected. You need to be very intentional about reclaiming your mind: it starts with self-education. Reclaiming expands when you connect with like-minded Black people. If you already participate in monthly activities with book-club friends, neighbors, or church members, you might be able to do even more with this group and on a more meaningful level. Commit to historical tours in your community and then expand to nearby cities and beyond. Identify annual festivals that highlight Black culture. Identify a Black woman from the Civil Rights Movement and learn all you can about her. Share this activity with your children and your nieces and nephews. The church hour doesn't have to be the only time that you come together with a deeper purpose. Perhaps your group can dedicate one day on the first Saturday of each quarter (January, April, July, October) to engage in a purposeful activity that deepens your connection to who you are.

Start now by creating a list of your first four activities. For example, research Black history activities in your local community. If there are few options, extend your search to the nearest larger city.

____

____

____

____

So much of "us" is stirred up simply in our togetherness. During card games, dominoes, and an impromptu Electric Slide, the joy of our culture cannot be denied. It doesn't really take a lot to create the vibe you need. We can reclaim an even deeper and enduring level of Black joy by *re*discovering who we are, together. Doing so raises your PF to a level that protects you from people and circumstances that would otherwise bring you down.

When you're with those who "get it," take time to talk about activities that you have wanted to do, but prefer to have someone participate with you. When your "recruits" are ready, follow some of these leads as you work collectively to claim a different future or ask them to be accountable with you, checking in to hear about what activities your family committed to doing:

Participate in traditions. If you do not have a tradition that affirms your Africanness, be creative. Some celebrate Kwanzaa annually beginning on December 26 through New Year's Day. If your family has not previously participated in a Juneteeth festival, it could be a meaningful annual event. What additional traditions inspire your participation?

____

____

____

____

Immerse yourself in culture. Take advantage of opportunities that exist in your community. Go to the local African American history museum and other Black cultural institutions. These institutions and their programming hold so many rich and empowering messages about who we are and the traditions of achievement and creativity that got us here, that just walking through one of their doors has the potential of raising your psychological fortitude by a noticeable measure. Most cities offer culturally immersive experiences. Seek them out in your town and list them here.

Make vacations meaningful. Plan your family vacations around visiting cultural experiences in other parts of the country. Invite other families. The National Museum of African American Culture and History in Washington, DC, is an excellent family destination. When you visit the National Museum, if you can, avoid going on a holiday so you can truly sit with the experience. Spend time on the bottom floors, which are devoted to our historical journey to freedom from the Middle Passage up to the present. Notice the details that you knew but also recognize the strength of those people. That strength is in you. Recognize that strength in you that is your responsibility to use to help Black people. Where have you wanted to go?

Engage with groups. It annoys me when white people get upset about us having our own organizations and clubs. They have no idea what it is like to be misrepresented or outright ignored, bombarded with messages that we do not belong, and devalued as lesser than someone of European ancestry. You must be unapologetically active in connecting with people and with experiences that will affirm you. Doing so raises your psychological fortitude. What groups are in your area that you might check out?

____

____

____

____

Incorporate positive influences for children. Being at home with little ones means that you might find ways to incorporate images of Black people in their early socialization. Buy Black dolls with natural hair. If they do not exist at your favorite store, buy one on Etsy. Make sure that you have Black History Flashcards available to practice learning about accomplishments that served to advance our society. In the presence of your children, be conscious of the way in which you talk about Black people in your family and in the media. If you allow your little ones to consume mainstream television, counter the negative and incorrect narratives about Black culture and behavior. How can you offer your children a home that supports Black culture?

____

____

____

____

Avoid demeaning TV shows. The ignorance that women are exposed to when they see Black women fighting on television is not conducive to your well-being. Such programming is demeaning. It is bad enough that non-Black people are entertained by how we mistreat each other. It is even worse when we are entertained by and participate in it. By now, I hope, you are beginning to think differently about who you are. You see the need to take a more intentional route to improving your PF and protecting that of your young son and daughter. They have to use their critical thinking skills to recognize Black empowerment versus efforts to undermine Black people. If there are no inspiring television shows available that you can relate to, maybe you will create one. No vision is too big. What media shows do you know to avoid? Why?

All in all, I want us to dream bigger than the American dream. Write your own future—one that does not hinge on how much of a white middle-class reality you can create for your daughter. It might somehow seem the easier route, but only because that route will encounter the least amount of resistance from the oppressor and those who are oppressed in the mind. Suicide occurs when there is no hope for the future. You can no longer be reactive to everyday discrimination and subtle messages that your voice and your existence are valueless. "America" will find ways to be what it has always been, so stop waiting for goodness to prevail. What if goodness is waiting for you to use your gifts to lift your own self up? Celebrate who you are. Under no circumstances can you reclaim your mind and obtain peak fortitude without embracing who you are or who you are to become. What is one big dream you have?

Wrap Up

You stand on too many shoulders to deny what your ancestors bring to the table. The same forces that propelled Shirley Chisholm, Maya Angelou, and Katherine Johnson are in you. Your ancestors used the worst parts of the pig to create meals that some now call delicacies. Those foods fed the hungry and saved lives. Be willing to think outside the box to create and pull from your culture what you need to thrive.

As a final caveat, connecting yourself and your family to your African cultural identity is not a substitute for getting treatment for your racial trauma symptoms, your severe worry, or your depression-induced sleep problems. It could help in the short term, but meaningful relief from these types of problems will be helped with very specific kinds of therapeutic intervention (see chapter 7).

Tapping into your cultural identity is a preventative boost. If you have a skin cancer, putting on sunblock is not going to fix it. The problem must first be eradicated. Then you can proceed to use protection from that which can do harm. Take care of your serious problems first. A high PF requires that you first prioritize taking the necessary steps to address these most pressing issues, and then you can proceed to cultivate your cultural protections.

CHAPTER 6

Get into Your Spiritual and Religious Rhythm

As you worked through the last chapter on strengthening resilience to contend with racism, thoughts about prayer and faith may have entered your mind. Like you, I'm convinced there's no way that folks can survive generations of oppression and now contemporary racism without belief in a Higher Power. Resilience and spiritual and religious resources go hand in hand. They are so important for your life that I wanted to dedicate a chapter to this topic. Unfortunately, conversations on religion and spirituality can get complicated quickly, but don't worry. We'll take time to unpack this conversation so you can elevate your religious and spiritual practice and boost your PF.

Distinguish Between Religiosity and Spirituality

Some experts think of religiosity as how we use our belief in a Higher Power to act, like going to church and reading the Bible regularly. Spirituality is how you choose to live a life of faith even if you are not religious. Many are spiritual but not religious. Interestingly, many who are religious also struggle with living a life of spirituality, connecting in meaningful ways to the peace of mind that comes from believing religious doctrine and knowing that sometimes you have to be still while God fight battles on our behalf.[19]

Dr. Jacqueline Mattis is a Rutgers University dean and expert in African American and Afro-Caribbean religiosity and spirituality. She has talked about spirituality as a relationship but also a "journey of self-reflection, self-criticism, and self-awareness that culminates in a greater understanding of the relationship between self, God, and the larger community (including the community of ancestors)."[20] She acknowledges the individual belief in and connection to metaphysical forces, including God and ancestral spirits. I especially like this definition because it speaks to a deep power within you. At the core of your African-centered culture is your spirituality. The opposite of this spiritual orientation is materialism or an emphasis on what you have and can get. It is okay to want that Range Rover. I am claiming one for myself one day. However, having peace in yourself, including a sense of who you are as a person of African ancestry, tapped into your greatest vision of your life, is what truly matters for your PF. And getting your religious practice in better focus can help.

Fortify Your Religious Foundation

Religion provides structure and organization for some people to channel spirituality and to know where to go, when to go, and what to do for spiritual connection when they get there. The actual religious service can be like group therapy. You show up along with others who have similarly overwhelming struggles, but you generally gain some sense of hope that things will turn out for the good.

In the following prompts, I want you to explore your own ideas about religion to gain some clarity. If you do not have a religious practice, consider skipping to item #5 below. Otherwise, find a quiet place. Take a few deep breaths to relax yourself before starting.

1. What does religious practice look like for you over the course of a typical week? This may include attending a religious service alone or with others, reading scripture, and so forth. Include an estimate of how frequently you engage in this practice (or practices) and as many other details about this experience as possible.

____

____

____

____

____

____

2. Can you recall a specific time when you ended a service (or practice) feeling especially inspired and motivated, as if you could take on the world? What do you recall about this day? How do you account for the "uplifting" you experienced?

____

____

____

____

____

____

3. Can you recall an especially low point in life when your church attendance or other religious activities were helpful? What was helpful on that occasion? If possible, revisit those activities (Is there a video recording for the day if a sermon took place?) to increase PF on an otherwise "ordinary" day.

4. Is there anything that keeps you from fully engaging in religious practice in ways that will help improve your PF? Perhaps you forget to read scriptural lessons. Perhaps you forget the pastor's inspiring message by the time someone upsets you in the parking lot. Are there limitations to your religious activities that you need to address?

5. Is there perhaps anything you'd like to revise about how you go about church or participate in other religious activities so they are more in line with what matters to you? Would you experiment with a new environment or find ways to become more involved where you already are?

6. It is understandable if you prefer not to engage in any religious practice. However, given the potential benefits and your struggles to sustain psychological fortitude, are there new ways that you can think about religiosity to build a regular practice for yourself? These might include reading Islamic texts, such as the Qur'an, or attending a Buddhist temple (making sure to first review expectations for etiquette).

Reflect on your responses to questions 4 through 6. You may need a mindset shift to ensure that your actions are truly consistent with what matters to you while also allowing for opportunities for greater psychological fortitude. The shift is about removing barriers and being open to what works for your PF. For some of us, church or another religious setting is the easiest place to connect with ourselves, community, and a Higher Power. In Black churches, you can be happy and cry, and feel something deep in your soul and not know why. Black folks who struggle all week need a "Word from the Lord." To get on a path that will help you connect to a Higher Power, you may want to find a place you can go to at least to get your rhythm going and to address specific concerns.

When you go to church, consider praying for guidance for what you need to do to resolve your difficult situation. You might ask God to put someone in your life who will help you meet your life goals or provide inspiration for what that path might look like. Maybe you'll hear a slight "whisper" of direction. Ask for the answer to be made plain to overcome your distracting and overactive mind.

Asking for Specific Help

Imagine you are sleep-deprived and chronically tired. You get five and a half hours of sleep on most nights. You might pray during a service to "get some rest." You can reframe a request such as this to "help me see the things that are keeping me up at night and come up with a solution to address the situation."

Now you try.

First, write down a current or recent emotional struggle that is negatively affecting your PF:

____

Now instead of asking for it to be gone and solved, try to reframe it in the most practical and helpful way possible.

____

If it is difficult to do this when thinking of yourself, let's try as if you were helping a friend with a work situation. Your friend says she is stressed out at work. Since the COVID pandemic, management has changed multiple times, there are a lot of new policies, and other employees don't want to work, so your friend has to take up the slack. She doesn't even enjoy the work anymore and is thinking of going back to school. She tells you that she is praying for *things to change at work*.

How might you help her reframe her prayer for specific action that she can pursue?

____

____

____

Now that you have prayed for your friend, let's revisit this activity for yourself. What specific prayers might you need for yourself?

____

____

____

____

I hope that in this exercise, you can see a way to make religious resources work for you.

Cultivate Active Faith

As a psychologist, I appreciate how biblical scriptures can line up with psychological interventions. For example, Romans 12:2 suggests that you can be "transformed by the renewing of your mind" and that life experiences will shift once you embrace a different way of thinking.[21]

There is a biblical scripture that says, "Faith without works is dead."[22] You may need to pray every day and also work on a step-by-step plan for yourself. Then, put your plan in motion or problem-solve what is keeping you from putting your plan in motion. Keep in mind that if prayer does not seem to be working, maybe your Higher Power is waiting for you to do something different.

Find Helpful Scriptures

I recall a time when I was working *extra* hard at a persistent difficulty in my marriage. One day, the preacher talked about how the Lord would fight for me. Since what I was doing wasn't working, I needed to take my hands off the wheel and shift my energy and efforts. When I shifted, the situation shifted (for the better!).

Think about some of your favorite scriptures—the ones that shift your perspective when you are most in need. Write them down.

What do you find most helpful about these scriptures?

Another Tip: Make a list of your favorite scriptures for "when I feel lonely" or "when I need encouragement" or whatever you feel you need most often. After a while, the scripture will become ingrained in your memory.

Think of your specific need (hope, confidence, rest).

What is a scripture that you found for that need?

Be mindful that your favorite scripture doesn't encourage you to simply be passive about your PF. If it makes you feel like an active participant in your own well-being, then write it down somewhere you will see it often. Make it your home screen on your phone or put a sticky note on your bathroom mirror.

Maybe scriptures aren't your thing. As another psychological fortitude tool, you can identify gospel songs that are particularly moving to you. When you get off from a long day of work and anticipate getting dinner together while navigating homework that you half understand, it could be a good boost to your fortitude to play your favorite song before you get out of the car. When you find yourself particularly disconnected and "off," music may be able to bring you to where you need to be. There are two things you can do that would be easy.

1. Create a playlist of your favorite gospel songs. One of my all-time favorites is the old-school "That's When You Bless Me" by LA Mass Choir. Also, Avery Sunshine's performance of "Safe in His Arms" always stops me in my tracks. You might include a traditional hymn, such as "I Need Thee Every Hour" or "Never Would Have Made It" with Le'Andria Johnson, for something more contemporary. When things aren't going your way, "I Won't Complain" by Rev. Paul Jones, "Grateful" by Hezekiah Walker, or any gospel song performed by Fantasia Barrino are all good options.

Brainstorm songs for your playlist here:

1. ______________________________
2. ______________________________
3. ______________________________
4. ______________________________
5. ______________________________
6. ______________________________
7. ______________________________
8. ______________________________
9. ______________________________
10. ______________________________

If you do not use Spotify, watch a quick video on how it works or simply save your songs in your YouTube account for easy access. Whatever you need to do to maintain an accessible playlist will be well worth the effort to reset your mood when things aren't going your way. What's key is setting up the playlist when you're already in a good mood.

2. Think of any specific ideas that you tap into when you are struggling. For example, many churches preach that God loves you unconditionally and that "no weapon formed against you will prosper." What are three regular teachings within your church that you can draw on?

1. ______________________________

____

____

____

2. ______________________________

____

____

____

3. ______________________________

____

____

____

It may very well be that your religious activities are satisfying your PF needs. Even so, there might be additional spiritual resources at your disposal that can also have profound effects on your PF. Too often, we don't realize that "church" alone is ineffective because we pretend to leave challenges "at the altar," but they follow us home.

Spirituality and Next-Level Psychological Fortitude

Have you ever had an overwhelmingly positive experience that you couldn't quite explain? Something that couldn't be accounted for by your own hard work and effort? Did you get a promotion that you didn't expect? Maybe a nice bonus came your way. Perhaps you caught a big break toward your next boss move. What did you attribute that to?

Paulo Coehlo, an internationally renowned, bestselling author, famously wrote, "When you want something, the whole universe conspires in order for you to achieve it."[23] You and your spirit are connected to the greater universe and your Higher Power. When you are spiritually tuned in, you are better able to recognize and achieve your life purpose. The pursuit of that purpose (rather than going through the motions of life) is part of your greater peace of mind.

When you are spiritually disconnected, you may be inclined to do nothing but wait on the Lord *or* "problem-solve" your way out of persistently stressful situations. You're an intelligent person. You've accomplished a few things in your life. In fact, it's probably your intuition and the "little voice" in your head that has gotten you as far as you've come. But somehow you forgot that you are connected to a greater universe. If you've been struggling for a while, it's time to strengthen your relationship with your Higher Power. It's understandable if you hadn't thought of this before now. Sometimes, life is on autopilot. You can keep doing what you're doing, but the longer you wait, the longer you'll be disconnected from your life purpose.

For your PF to reach its highest potential, you have to boost your spiritual well-being and devote time for self-reflection. Because all you need in this process is you and your quiet mind, the opportunities are endless.

You have access to a Higher Power that is always available and will always guide you in the right direction as long as you take time to listen. Your religious participation, together with your spirituality, has likely given you hope in tough times as well as reassurance that you are not alone. It is time to push things further. The inner voice that comes with a strong spiritual self has the power to make a way out of no way. It expands your possibilities in work, relationships, and overall health and motivates you to instill practical habits to relieve stress and stay focused on your values and life purpose.

Explore Your Spirituality

Are there any spiritual practices you engage in, like meditation, prayer, deep breathing, yoga, pouring libation, or others, in a private space? What, if anything, have these practices brought to your life?

What texts inspire you? Have writings of Iyanla Vanzant, Sarah Jakes Roberts, or others inspired you to look deep into yourself?

Are there regular practices or rituals that you participate in (like daily prayers or candle burning) that you find joyful or bring you a positive sense of purpose and connection?

Do you devote adequate time to listening and therefore to nurturing your spirit voice, also known as the "little voice" that aims to guide you?

If you have yet to develop a practice, imagine what you would want it to look like, including times of day and where you would be. Create your vision here.

Religion and Spirituality on the Shelf Is Not the Answer

There are moments that you feel fully empowered to withstand your enemies. Unfortunately, those moments aren't sustained, perhaps because meaningful change is needed. We don't need church to *feel* better but otherwise remain the same—same thoughts, same behavior, and same outcome. Something about how you think and what you do needs to fundamentally change as a result of your Sunday or Wednesday-night participation. Your spiritual connection outside of these activities is how you raise your PF.

Sometimes, when you go to church or other place of "worship," it is for much needed inspiration and sometimes out of desperation. You feel better but resume your regularly scheduled programming.

Though some pastors are psychologically savvy, a rare few have formal mental health training. Your pastor can counsel you on how you are on the wrong path and how you can pray and fast to deal with your distress. Your pastor's sermon may challenge you to not "lean unto your own understanding,"[24] despite how intelligent and upwardly mobile you are. This is all very important. However, if you need to get out from under crippling anxiety, there are specific strategies and tools for that. If you are exhausted but do not sleep at night because you keep waking up with stuff on your mind and cannot go back to sleep, there is help for that. Pray for specific solutions. Tap into your spiritual strength to secure change in your life.

During the first few years of my doctoral program, I struggled so much with my primary advisor that I made moves to quit after three years in the program. It made no sense to me that I was earning a PhD in clinical psychology to help others, but I felt I was losing my mind in the process. Without going into details, trust me when I say that the advisor is the single most important person (other than the student) in obtaining the doctoral degree. I prayed for guidance and did all that I could to satisfy the advisor, but nothing seemed to work (or nothing that I could see!). As I was finalizing my departure, a wise friend and fellow student recommended that I talk to a new faculty member about being my advisor. I didn't have in mind to ask the new advisor in part because he was quite intimidating. My friend pointed out that I had nothing to lose. She was right. The universe was conspiring for my success.

You forfeit your natural gifts when you don't trust and believe in your Higher Power and your connection to that power. If you have been saying that you are "waiting on the Lord," the reality is that much of your suffering and low PF will also continue to wait. It can feel tricky to know when to wait and when to make a move, but if life is making no sense, you have a decision to make.

There seems to be conflicting biblical messaging about waiting and working, but you must hear the message and *apply* the text or whatever the guidance is to your life. If your situationship or your job is not working for you, something has to change. You insist on staying in your miserable, but familiar, job to wait on the Lord, but your waiting could be a crutch. These messages have tremendous power to help us, but you have to first adopt a mindset to act on behalf of your own well-being. What if you used what you learned on Sunday morning to change rather than to endure?

Is there anything that you need to stop waiting for?

____

____

____

How can you act on behalf of your own well-being?

____

____

____

Consider this: Do you think that you were created to be miserable? Being spiritual does not mean suffering indefinitely with severe depression. I understand that part of how depression works is that it steals your energy and willpower. Depression and anxiety can paralyze you to the idea of making a plan and following through with it. If this is the case, take small steps, such as drafting a vision for what you want to be different or setting a day and time to reach out for help to address these challenges, but resist the urge to blame biblical scripture or the pastor's sermon for all of your inaction. If you are not ready for change, it really is OK to accept this hard truth. You will be ready in time.

Wrap Up

Having access to a Higher Power is important because you are not going to be able to survive everything that comes at you without a strong dose of spirituality. I encourage you to explore a spirituality that you can access at any time and that reveals to you how powerfully special you are.

Think of your spirituality especially in those moments of greatest challenge. You have to make a decision that your happiness is yours as long as you claim it. Spend time deciding what would be important to you if you were not trying to confirm to someone else's expectations of you. Seek spiritual discernment through prayer and meditation. Discernment requires focus, but it is a tuning in to your own spirit that strengthens as you use it.

You will need to access your spiritual self to overcome those unhelpful thoughts that say your situation and future are hopeless. The tools you've learned in this book so far are your first lines of defense against low PF. Once your new skills get you to a place of more sustained authenticity and peace, access your spirituality to amplify the most powerful parts of yourself.

CHAPTER 7

Your Questions About Therapy Answered

When prayer, meditation, churchgoing, journaling, spiritual rituals, and everything else that you tried have been insufficient for you to shake what ails you, you may need professional mental health services or counseling. Think of it as a professional "collaboration" with someone who can help you fix the shortcomings of your current tools and tailor them to you. You may benefit from a shorter-term fix, or you may have a more serious problem on hand. If you are ready to consider seeking a therapist, psychiatrist, or other mental health professional, I want to remind you from the outset that this is a journey. I know also that while therapy can be very helpful, you may have so many "but what about this...or that..." questions that cause you to procrastinate on your decision to explore therapy for months or years. When you find the right professional to help you make your way to wellness, all the effort is well worth it. To get you on your way, I'll answer the common questions I am asked.

Isn't therapy for white people?

It's true, emotional health care is not necessarily designed with Black people in mind. There have been some efforts to be more inclusive of your needs and to advance "cultural competence." Most accredited programs, at least in psychology, embrace cultural competence as an objective. That means that students in training take a course or two in multicultural psychology and are expected to be able to successfully navigate the nuances of working with clients who are Black, Asian, Latinx/Hispanic, LGBTQ2, or have few financial resources—any reality that impacts how the client experiences the world that is not a mainstream, middle-class, Eurocentric lens. For some, a course or two with practice seeing clients from diverse backgrounds to supplement their personal knowledge of different groups is sufficient. But there is much more work to be done. You can, nevertheless, benefit from learning tools and strategies that help with common problems that many people face. These include communication challenges in romantic relationships and sexism that women experience at work.

If I talk about my worries and fears, will other people find out?

A lot of people are afraid that once they tell the therapist their "business," it will get out. Therapists have an ethical responsibility to confidentiality. Anyone who is a licensed practitioner has an ethical obligation to maintain the client's confidentiality. Confidentiality includes not just the contents of what you are discussing while in therapy, but often the fact that you are in therapy. For example, it is common that therapists will not acknowledge their clients if they run into them outside of therapy in an effort to protect a client's confidentiality. Other ways you can count that the therapist is protecting your confidentiality include:

- Not leaving revealing information on voicemail or text
- Not acknowledging to outside parties that a client has an appointment
- Not discussing the contents of therapy with a third party, such as a family member or employer, without the explicit permission of the client.

There are a few exceptions. If your therapist feels you are in danger or a danger to others, they are required to notify the appropriate third party. An exception also applies to victims of abuse—particularly children.

I'm still functioning, so why go to therapy?

You don't have to be crazy or on the verge of an emotional breakdown to be in therapy. You do not have to have a serious problem with depression, anxiety and fear, or alcohol addiction to get help. It's best to get help *before* you're in crisis because waiting for things to break down means that it'll be much harder to get back on track.

Reasons to start therapy can be varied and range from difficulty sleeping to persistent unwanted intrusive thoughts. Additionally, fear of future outcomes or an inability to process grief are other reasons people begin therapy. Use your intuition when you don't feel like yourself. Hopefully, this book gives you improved self-awareness, and when things feel off—that PF rating getting and staying at 5 or lower for whatever reason—you recognize these are indications that you might benefit from therapy.

Also it's important to be on watch for beliefs that *Black people don't go to therapy* or *Only weak people go to therapy* and how that mindset plays out into your ideas about therapy. *I'm still functioning* can sometimes be a setup to *pretend* to "be strong" when the reality is that being strong can go only so far.

What if the therapist decides I should be "locked up"?

You might be afraid that if people find out how bad off you are, you risk being "locked up." People of color are overrepresented in long-term mental health care, but the mental health landscape is much different now. A very high burden of proof is needed for forced hospitalization. Even if you share suicidal thoughts with a therapist, that alone isn't grounds to put you away for treatment. If you are believed to be in *imminent* danger of hurting yourself or others, you could be hospitalized, but imminent danger requires a great deal of certainty. Even then, any hospitalization would last for only a few days. Anyone who is in that type of danger likely needs a few days to get help and reset, mentally.

Are all therapists the same? Does it matter who I see?

Even if a therapist did good work with your best friend, she might not be a good match for you because of your different challenges or your different personality. Different therapists approach the therapeutic relationship in different ways. Some therapists are very active in session and talk frequently, while others take a more passive or nondirective role in session. More passive therapists may listen and nod, but not talk as much. So it's important to ask yourself whether the therapist's approach fits you and your needs. By necessity, therapy isn't always easy or enjoyable—it often requires facing up to painful difficulties and life patterns. So it's essential that the person companioning you on your therapy journey be someone you respect and who you feel truly "gets" you or that they get you enough that you feel comfortable and "heard" by them. Like medical doctors, psychotherapists have areas of expertise. Although most therapists are legally licensed to treat a wide variety of clients and issues, this doesn't mean all therapists are equally good at everything.

Additionally, certain problems require more frequent therapy meetings than others, and some people may value a higher level of availability in their therapist than other people. Nonetheless, clients rarely consider this factor when choosing a provider. Some therapists, for instance, work in small private practices where their ability to take spontaneous phone calls or set up extra meetings may be severely limited. Others may work in large clinics that offer 24/7 crisis hotlines and the availability of group therapy in addition to regular one-on-one weekly meetings. If you think you'll need more intensive therapy than a once-a-week session can afford, it's worth bringing this up with potential therapists before committing to treatment.

Can I work with a Black therapist?

You may have questions to consider for yourself. In a perfect world and if you prefer one, you will find a Black therapist who is well trained in providing mental health services and dedicated to elevating your psychological fortitude. Because therapy relationships are so important, you may wonder if you can only trust and be comfortable with a Black therapist. This feeling is absolutely understandable. You would not want to subject yourself to yet another space where you have to pretend to not be you, you avoid your African American Vernacular to speak Standard English, or even worse, your therapist acts like she doesn't see you as Black. Finding a Black therapist might be ideal. But race is not the only criteria, or the most important, for you to consider. Your Black therapist might be nice, but if she has no experience with evidence-based interventions for trauma, for example, your capacity to improve will be limited. The therapy might feel good because she is a great listener in a way that no one else in your life listens, but you won't address the trouble that your trauma has been causing you.

Is seeing a white therapist ever a good idea?

There are white therapists who are perfectly fine seeing a Black client. This is important because when you are struggling emotionally, the last thing that you want to do is see a therapist who is uncomfortable around Black people. However, I assure you that there are therapists out there who would be good at establishing a relationship with you. You are best served if you do your homework, get reliable referrals, and research your options.

As you might expect, most therapists are white women. The mental health system is, in many ways, a microcosm of our larger society. Not everyone is "culturally competent" and able to demonstrate their ability to work with individuals who are culturally different from them.

If you find that a white therapist may be your only option, you can assess whether or not that person could be a good fit for you. Ask what percentage of her clients have been African American or Black or who are first-generation United States citizens. If the question elicits discomfort, that might be all the data you need to move on to the next potential therapist on your list.

You want to know that your provider will be genuinely receptive when you give her feedback about her interactions with you. Therapists who aspire to cultural humility are willing to be critical of themselves. They are flexible and willing to learn more about you and, importantly, what your culture means to you.

How do I find a therapist?

Finding an effective therapist is no easy process. I do, however, have some suggestions that you might not have considered for finding the right person for you. I share them in the questions to come and also in the "Resources" at the end of the book.

Might my employer be a resource?

To find an individual therapist, you may be surprised to know that your employer can help. Two ways to get referrals through your job are through employee assistance programs and health insurance providers. An employee assistance program (EAP) is a voluntary program offered through an employer that provides employees free and confidential assessments, short-term counseling, referrals, and follow-up services for their personal and work-related problems. Most programs provide counselors who are equipped to address issues affecting mental and emotional well-being like the ones that we have been discussing. Admittedly, I rarely hear of anyone contacting their job's EAP for referrals, but I once met an African American woman who did just that. She was very pleased with the services that she received. Too often, the EAP is underutilized perhaps because of fears related to privacy. However, the EAP-recommended therapist is bound to confidentiality as is any licensed professional. If you have questions or concerns, be sure to bring them up with the therapist.

Can I go through my health insurance?

Your company's health insurance provider is another job-based resource. You may have mental health coverage, and if you do, the health insurance company will likely provide a list of mental health providers. This information is often accessible online. This is another option to get you started.

How do I search for a therapist?

There are several internet search options that you can conduct to find a therapist. Numerous online resources detail the various types of mental health professionals. You want to look or ask specifically for "psychotherapists." If you just search "therapist," that person could actually be offering another kind of therapy, such as occupational therapy or physical therapy. The search for "counselor" typically works but is also quite broad. Your pastor is also a counselor but will not likely have training in psychotherapy. A psychotherapist provides therapy for the mind and behavior.

Are there websites you recommend to find a therapist?

Therapy for Black Girls, http://www.therapyforblackgirls.com, is one resource. Therapists provide contact information along with a photograph and brief description of their expertise. The site is not comprehensive, but many Black and African American therapists from across the United States have signed on to the directory.

The Black Girl Doctor, http://www.theblackgirldoctor.com/, is another resource designed with Black women in mind. Providers are all psychologists who provide mental health care or coaching in more than thirty states. Their experience and credentials are detailed on the site.

Psychology Today magazine, http://www.psychologytoday.com/us/therapists, also provides a directory of therapists with photos and detailed credentialing. The site provides a stamp for therapists in their directory whose name, license, and contact information have been verified. Though the institution where the individual obtained the degree is listed, this information is not verified. You can verify any therapist's credentials by searching online for the state licensing board. If the person is a psychologist in Decatur, Georgia, you can search online for "psychology licensing board Georgia." For a licensed professional counselor, search "licensing board counseling Georgia." You will be able to verify the individual's license and also whether or not any complaints have been filed.

The American Psychological Association also has a psychologist locator, http://locator.apa.org. Only members of the American Psychological Association (who are presumably licensed psychologists) can be listed in the directory. Similar to the other sites, profiles include photos and areas of expertise along with contact information.

Though it is not a well-known option for mental health care, many large research universities have psychological clinics on campus that provide care to people in the community through doctoral student psychologists in training. We recently had a client leave our clinic because his mother thought he should see "a psychologist." Unfortunately, she did not understand that our therapists are psychologists in training who are supervised by licensed psychologists or doctoral-level professors and provide affordable, cutting-edge care that is evidence-based. Because the doctoral student therapists are in training with other students, their clients benefit from the team of students and their doctoral-level professor who work together to develop the treatment plan.

What do all those credentials mean?

Some therapists have doctoral degrees. Others have master's degrees. All must be licensed to practice in the state where they provide service, meaning that, in addition to having the degree, they must pass national and state exams and participate in continuing education. The variety of credentials illustrate that there are different areas of expertise and approaches to training. Nevertheless, all therapists are expected to obtain a license to practice ethically. If you see your therapist in person, the license should be visible to you in their office.

Most available practitioners have master's level degrees. They may be licensed professional counselors (LPC) and licensed mental health counselors (LMHC) or obtain licensure as an MFT, a marriage and family therapist. These individuals have completed master's-degree-level coursework in psychology, counseling, or marriage and family therapy and obtained the required number of supervised clinical hours before being authorized to see clients independently. Licensed clinical social workers (LCSW) are also credentialed at the master's degree level and provide individual, family, and group therapy. Psychiatric nurse practitioners provide mental health services and are often affiliated with a medical center or hospital. There are providers who specialize in treatment of substance-use problems who may not have graduate degrees but have earned a certification to practice.

Should my therapist have a doctoral degree?

Your needs and preferences will determine who is the most qualified professional for you. Licensed psychologists have typically earned doctoral-level PhDs or PsyDs. PhD programs in psychology are highly competitive and require that students balance learning skills to work with psychotherapy clients and understanding and developing research (whereby they are immersed in the science of mental health). PsyD programs primarily emphasize expertise in psychological testing and psychotherapy, though some also engage in research.

What's with all the different approaches to therapy?

All therapists are not equal. Also, all therapies are not equal and will not achieve the same results.. Researchers have determined that given certain types of problems, certain therapies are much more effective than others. In evidence-based practice (EBP), psychological scientists have tested different approaches to specific types of problems. I add a caveat here that some of these researchers have rarely if ever published research on the usefulness of an intervention with African Americans. However, if you consider a therapist who has expertise in treating a certain type of problem that has been debilitating for you, you can ask if she uses EBP and if not, what her approach is. I can say with confidence that if you have been managing depression most days of the week for many months, an evidence-based intervention is the best option for you. For depression, evidence-based therapies seem to have longer-lasting effects than medication alone. If you have not been able to heal yourself from social anxiety, evidence-based practice that involves "exposure" is the best approach.

Cognitive behavioral therapy, or CBT, is my preferred approach to addressing life challenges. If you're experiencing excessive worry, problems sleeping, overeating, and even unexplained pain in your body, there is a CBT intervention. Because depression and anxiety are the most commonly occurring psychological problems, they have the most developed interventions—these would include things like cognitive restructuring, exposure, and mindfulness practice. Preliminary research has found that mindfulness and newer "third-wave" treatments are helpful. Common third-wave therapies that you may have heard of are acceptance and commitment therapy (good for existential issues), dialectical behavior therapy (good for emotional overwhelm), and behavioral activation (good for depression). Though some of the work is preliminary, I have observed situations in which general mindfulness exercises helped clients alleviate lingering symptoms of depression when the benefits of CBT seemed to max out.

Keep in mind, however, that the therapist's treatment approach is meaningful but not nearly as important as their connection with you. You are the center of the decision when it comes to selecting a therapist.

Can I find a therapist for a specific problem I'm having?

Depending on their training, most therapists can assist you in developing tools to manage life stress. However, some therapists have expertise in specific areas. These could be anything from addressing trauma-related relationship anxiety to integrating your spiritual beliefs in mindfulness-based therapies. Therapists also undergo training to specialize in suicide prevention, marriage and family counseling, and nicotine and other addictions. If you see someone for a specific psychological disorder for which they are not trained to use evidence-based practice, you may walk away dissatisfied. Because of the delicate nature of trauma and traumatic responses, I would advise that you find someone who has expertise with EBP in that area. Advising you to "not think about it" is never helpful.

What's the difference between a psychiatrist and a psychologist?

The distinction between psychiatrists and psychologists is important to your search for therapy versus medication and other medical interventions. Psychiatrists are doctors of medicine (MDs) who prescribe medication, while psychologists typically earn PhDs and engage in talk therapy. Psychiatrists are specifically trained in the use of medicine to improve mental health. Medications, such as Xanax, that influence brain functioning are known as "psychotropics." Some psychiatrists also provide talk therapy, but the majority do not. In most states, psychologists cannot prescribe medications. I'll answer common questions about medication soon.

Can I explore different therapists or meet them first?

In some ways, finding a therapist can be a dice roll, but review their personal web profiles for their expertise and what they offer to clients. It may also take some of the pressure off your search if you know that the provider that you begin with may not be the provider you end up with. Once you decide you want professional help, you may have little time or energy for shopping around. However, you are not bound to stay with a therapist in the same way that you are not bound to stay with a physician who is not meeting your needs. Make a list of at least three possible therapist options from the start. You might schedule a phone conversation or initial session with all three, or you might schedule the initial session with one to see how it goes and plan to schedule with the next if the first session feels lukewarm or like a poor fit in your first encounter with a new therapist. During your initial meeting, ask the therapist about their approach and perspective on therapy. You could even use the information covered in this chapter to direct your questions.

How does a therapist get me to open up? Am I supposed to just trust them right out of the gate?

If you have never been in therapy before, you may not know what to expect. Know also that therapists are expected to be affirming and nonjudgmental, but each therapist has a different style and approach to therapy. This approach helps to build rapport and helps clients feel more comfortable sharing in session.

Rapport is the positive, trusting, working relationship between the therapist and the client that is at the foundation of therapy success. And it goes both ways. Your therapist should hold space for you and follow through on their commitment to helping you as much as you find ways to be vulnerable and open and honest with yourself and your therapist in session. But you can go at your own pace, building trust as time passes. All psychological science tells us that it is the most important (but not the only) factor in whether you are able to meet your therapy goals. The available science suggests that rapport is more important than therapist expertise.

If you rely on television and movies as your source of insight to how therapy goes, you may be misled. Though less-structured approaches to therapy do occur whereby the client shares their current challenges and the therapist asks follow-up questions for clarification and offers guidance or a different perspective, structured approaches are more effective.

What can I expect as I begin?

In the very first session of a structured therapy, your new therapist begins by discussing confidentiality and limits to confidentiality, expectations about cancellations, and other logistics. In the first session, the therapist will also ask you for background information (what type of work you do, level of education, living situation, and so on). They will ask what it is that brings you in for therapy. Also in the first session, the therapist talks to you about their approach to therapy. The agenda for future sessions will depend on your goals for therapy and the therapist's approach. The amount of information that the therapist shares about themselves will vary but will be relatively limited in the interest of focusing more on you. If you prefer to ask questions of the therapist to feel more comfortable, you can do so. Write down any questions you want to ask the therapist here.

____

____

____

____

How long will this take?

It is hard to know how long therapy will take, but to be sure, it is unlikely that any actual "change" would take place in the first session. However, the therapist may ask you questions that will cause you to seriously evaluate your life situation and give you a different perspective and inspiring new insight. Over the course of therapy, you and your therapist will work together to address the unhappiness that brought you to therapy. You'll do so in a way that makes sense to you. At agreed-upon intervals, you can evaluate how things are going. For therapy in general, plan on no less than twelve sessions, but this depends on your level of distress and your willingness to work on assigned tasks outside session.

How can I make the most of therapy?

To be most effective, you will want to be as open as you can possibly be so the therapist understands the true nature of your problems. You will also want to complete any assignments, tasks, or homework that the therapist advises.

It is important to keep top of mind your "why" of therapy. That is, how would you want your life to be different at the end of the therapy journey? If you have a lot going on, you can be sidetracked by the "stress of the day," but if you focus on your overall goal (or perhaps how your daily situations are connected to your goal), you will have more success. You are taking an important and profound step toward improving your well-being and maintaining a high PF. Thus, the therapeutic journey is entwined with your commitment to yourself and your health. Being present with this attitude of self-care will lead to good outcomes.

Can medication actually help me?

Prescription medication can help you get out of a rut so you can benefit from therapy. A chemical imbalance is difficult to overcome with willpower alone. If you have been in therapy for months or years with tremendous difficulty achieving small goals despite having a well-trained therapist, there is a chance that you could benefit from medication.

You may not need medication, but if you do, it is best prescribed and managed by a psychiatrist. They can work with you to figure out if an antidepressant, antianxiety, or other psychotropic prescription could be helpful for you. Your primary care physician can also prescribe medication. However, navigating psychotropic medication can be a delicate process. There are various medications that could have different side effects. The doctor will do their best to find the right medication type for you.

Who lets me know if medication might help?

There are a number of different types of medication, or "psychotropics." A psychiatrist would be best equipped to consider alternative psychotropics and the appropriate dosage. Also, if you are on other medications, the psychiatrist can problem-solve if your medications are impacting one another.

If you are just beginning to think about improving your psychological fortitude and strongly dislike medications, it is okay to begin with "talk therapy," whereby you work through your problems with a psychologist or licensed professional counselor. Sometimes, psychologists will recommend the addition of medication to your regimen after a period of time. There is no quick fix for real, lasting change. Please commit to challenging your biases so you can make the best decision for your health and well-being. When it comes to your very complex psychological fortitude, the perfect formula—which could include medication—may take some time to figure out. You might as well put some effort toward finding a solution.

What if there are side effects to the medication?

If you are tempted to stop taking your prescription after one week, let the professional who prescribed the medication know about the uncomfortable side effects. Call their office and speak to the nurse. Do not keep your experience to yourself and simply discontinue your medication. Take time to figure out what works for you by working with your health professionals.

I want to feel better yesterday. When will therapy start to work?

Therapy is not magical. It does not work overnight. If you go into a session thinking that you will be healed of your ills inside of two weeks, you will be disappointed. When you decide to see a professional, you may be at the height of distress or at your lowest psychological fortitude. The therapist's first responsibility is to establish a relationship with you and gain some insight about what is going on for you, how the problem came to be, and what you have done to manage it.

Sometimes the problem came to be over decades. The therapist may have to uncover decades of hurt to understand your current problem. Often after you address one problem, another seems to emerge unexpectedly.

You know you're making progress over time when you gain new insights, regularly use your new skills, and begin to feel better. You will have a sense of alleviation from what brought you to therapy.

Life may feel less tiring and burdensome in multiple areas because the process of pausing, assessing your emotions, interrogating your thoughts, and building new behavior pathways helps you exist more in line with the kind of person you want to be and live the life you want to live. You do, however, have to identify specific goals "beyond feeling better." A specific goal looks like "I want to have PF at 7 or higher rather than 5 and lower on most days," or "I want to manage my anxiety so I no longer have panic attacks." Given specific goals, your therapist will also ask questions to assess how you are doing and perhaps provide you with specific questionnaires so they have numerical scores—like your PF—that show how your well-being is changing over time.

What if I don't feel like I'm making progress?

If there is a chance that you would not return to therapy with a specific therapist because you do not think they can help you, it is best that you let the therapist know up front. In doing so, the therapist can take time to determine what might be done to fix your most pressing problem (because there is often more than one) or let you know what additional information is needed to address that problem. In any case, follow your instincts. If you do not feel comfortable with the therapist, you can let them know that it is not working out. If you are comfortable, but feeling antsy, you may want to settle in for a while. Many of the reasons for a low PF are learned thoughts and behaviors that have rooted in us our whole life. Digging up those roots can take time. Also, remember that starting therapy is a single step on a journey.

I hope I've addressed your questions—especially if they've been stopping you from seeking professional support. With all this in mind, write down any lingering questions you may have. Whether you want to know what can help most for your diagnosis, what you can say to family or friends who are considering therapy (if anything at all), or what is happening in research on mental health care for Black people's needs, write down anything that's still on your mind.

____

____

____

____

____

Wrap Up

Sometimes our lingering but vague questions can paralyze us—asking questions can help put them in perspective and lead to finding answers. Try searching online, in private mode if that helps you must. Or ask a therapist on an initial visit. Unfortunately, the mental health system can be daunting. If you want individual help navigating a complex mental health care system to get what you need for yourself and those you care about, you can contact them to ask your additional, specific questions.

CHAPTER 8

Caring for Struggling Loved Ones

Are you someone who wants to help a loved one or someone you care about? Perhaps that person is struggling with making change in their own life. Perhaps that individual is resistant to making change for one reason or another. If you have been inspired by "unapologetic" strategies and a new perspective that have increased your psychological fortitude, you may be eager to help others. You are to be applauded for hoping to share your new insight to facilitate change for others.

A key step to helping someone is meeting them. Where. They. Are. Too often, we assume that we know how to help or assume we know the individual wants help and what they need. One of the single most common questions that I get is "How can I help someone who needs help?" This question has an implied judgment that the person needs help. The funny thing is that they are asking me because they either know or suspect that the individual doesn't realize the depth of their issues or the individual is outwardly denying that they have any issues.

At the other end of the spectrum, we presume that the person in need is so "bad off" that we do not have what it takes to be supportive. We fear we could do more harm than good. When you do offer "help," you advise that the situation isn't that bad or (even worse) that it's not as stressful as a situation that you once went through. In any case, you attempt to manage the situation by minimizing it either for yourself or for your loved one. You know (from reading about stages of change in chapter 4) that not everyone is ready for real change. There is, nevertheless, a role that you can play. You are part of a community that benefits from having *all hands on deck.* Begin with recognizing some ABC's of communication.

The ABC's are (1) assume you can help, (2) be a good listener, and (3) cancel your judgments.

Assume that you can help. Being present and available makes a difference for someone who feels isolated. It does not matter that you are not her best friend, that you haven't talked in months, or that you don't share your "personal business." Being present shows that you care. That means more than you know.

Be a good listener. Your loved one needs to connect even if they do not realize how much. You do not have to talk about their frustration of failing at work and in marriage. You can acknowledge that they are going through a tough time and that being upset is understandable. If you can, tell them about a time that they helped you personally. State what you value about them but perhaps haven't ever shared. Evidence that they matter will go a long way.

Cancel your judgments. You cannot be helpful if you're being judgmental, asking why they feel the way that they do, or trying to convince them that things aren't so bad. Try to suspend your personal values about whether something "should" be overwhelming. Other people's judgment is exactly why they do not talk about their problems. If you know that you like to judge people and tell them how to feel, revisit the previous point: be a good listener.

Typically, it's not wise to ask questions about someone's well-being unless you are prepared for whatever the answer may be. To be sure, we have normalized traditional but empty greetings of "How are you?" and routine responses of "I'm doing fine." These social interactions are so common that a different approach will take time to resonate broadly. Those around you, however, can expect your engaged inquiry. Using the skills you've learned here, rather than ask how they are doing, ask about their PF. You can use this script:

"I was listening to a wellness expert the other day. She talked about helpful ways to ask someone how they're doing. She suggested asking their psychological fortitude rating, or their ability to manage their lives. Managing life includes things like working, taking care of family, eating right, exercising, not letting emotions get overwhelming, living a life purpose, and being able to anticipate threats to doing well. She said you can rate all of that together between 0 and 10, with 0 being no ability to do those things and 10 being able to manage it all. Does that make sense?"

If they agree that it does, say: "If you had to give yourself a rating, what would it be?"

If the person gives a 5 or lower, let them know you're there for them however would be helpful—to talk about the most stressful thing they're managing or just to talk about anything they choose.

Here are five things you can say to or do for someone who might be going through a stressful or difficult situation.

1. Invite them out for lunch—let them know that you just want to brighten their day.
2. Message them a YouTube link for an upbeat song or a 90s playlist.
3. Have a flower or fruit arrangement delivered to their home.
4. Order a copy of one of your favorite inspirational books to be delivered to their home.
5. Offer to pick their child or children up from daycare or school and keep them through dinner time.
6. Send links for three restaurants and tell them to choose one for dinner in the next few days—your treat.

7. Hand-deliver a frozen meal with a note: "Thinking of you!"
8. Invite them to go with you for a pedicure.
9. Write them a letter that expresses what you admire about them.
10. Message them or leave a voice message: "If you give me until (insert specific time or day), I'm going to Facetime you or stop by" (or one of the nine ideas above). Whatever it is, be realistic so you can keep your promise.

Who is someone that comes to mind because they could use your help with a current or recent struggle that they have been having? Write their name here:

____

What do you see as the primary source of the difficulty?

____

____

____

What is it that you would want to do to support them?

____

____

Assuming that the individual hasn't invited your assistance, list two or three small gestures of support that you could implement.

____

____

____

____

____

Have you ever needed support and realized there was no one there for you? If you are having a challenging time thinking of how to support your loved one, consider what you would like for someone to do for you if you're feeling overwhelmed. List three things that would be nice for someone to do for you but that you can do for someone else:

1. ______________________________

2. ______________________________

3. ______________________________

Tough Love...for You

If you think "tough love" is needed because they are not ready for support or help, try a firm form of love that could be tougher on you than it is on them—one that requires you to invest time and extends to them some grace. Communicate that you're not going anywhere and will be available whenever they need you. You can do this by scheduling a text to them every few days. It could be something as simple as "I just want you to know I'm here for you." To switch things up, you might say "I just saw ____, and it reminded me of the time we ____." Keep in mind that talking harshly to someone who is already struggling will not be helpful.

Think of a time that you helped someone who was in need. The need could have been big (like making a one-time loan to a family member who needed money to pay a bill) or small (like taking your child's neighborhood friend home after school when their mom had to work late).

Reflect on how you felt to do something that helped someone else in a stressful situation. Perhaps you got a small boost to your PF knowing that you helped them out of a serious bind.

____

____

____

____

____

____

Getting Help Is Hard

Unfortunately, there is sometimes *baggage* that can go along with receiving help. Your friend may not be ready for change. To accept help from you may be embarrassing because they feel like they "should" be able to handle their issues on their own. It could be that they are comfortable with the way things are even if they know it's not working. On the other hand, it could be that you have the best of intentions, but you accidentally offend your friend by minimizing what they are going through.

Receiving help is hard and can create resistance. Try to recall the last time that someone tried to get you to do something that you did not want to do even if it was for your good. What was that?

____

____

How did you feel about their insistence on offering their assistance or trying to get you to change?

____

____

Perhaps you did it, but with some anxiety or resentment. Perhaps you determined that you would avoid that individual in the future. Reflect on how the situation turned out in the end.

____

____

At the end of the day, you want to *build* your relationships rather than undermine them. When that individual is in a fix, you want to be someone who they feel safe asking for help.

For Someone Who Could Be Near Crisis

It is important for you to know that asking about or talking to someone about suicide will not make them suicidal. The research on this is consistent. They will not spontaneously come up with a suicide plan because you asked if they were considering suicide. However, someone who is thinking about ending their life could see your nonjudgmental question as a sign of care and concern for them.

If someone you know seems "off," it can be hard to know how to approach them or exactly what to say. Regardless of what you say or how they respond, know that your loved one's pain probably isn't about you. Their level of upset and anger or sadness is theirs. If they yell at you or refuse to disclose how they are feeling, don't take it personally.

If you think the individual could be in crisis, you cannot count on them to initiate contact with you, especially if you haven't laid any groundwork by checking on them. Also, would you ask someone with an unaddressed broken foot or ankle to go for a walk to get help? Probably not. You would go to them.

Ask generally: "What can I do to help?" Or more directly: "Are you thinking of hurting yourself?" If the answer to the latter is no, follow up: "If you weren't OK, would you tell me?" If they hesitate, tap into the ABC's of listening and prepare to be a patient listener.

Some signs of crisis are more or less obvious. The individual may talk about their circumstances being hopeless and not caring if they live or die. They may talk about feeling like their life has no purpose and they are only a burden to others. You might have noticed that they started engaging in impulsive behavior or they are not acting at all like themselves in the midst of overwhelming pain or grief. They may have withdrawn from loved ones and begun to seem chronically agitated and show difficulties relaxing. They may even use alcohol or illicit drugs and have frequent mood swings.

If you believe someone to be in serious danger, such that they might not live through the night or day or next few days without some intervention, it's important to call 911. When you call, let the emergency dispatcher know who you are in relation to the individual and what the situation is.

This can be a very difficult decision in light of over-policing in Black communities. It could be helpful to first call or text the Suicide and Crisis Lifeline (SMS 988) for guidance.

In any event, you can take responsibility for asking questions; listening to vulnerable friends, loved ones, and coworkers; and offering help as needed.

Has there ever been a time that you fell short in helping a friend or loved one? Perhaps you suspected "something was up" but you brushed it off? Maybe they asked for help, but you avoided giving them a response because you felt overwhelmed in your own life. Reflect on how you could have approached the situation differently. Was there a way that you could have been responsive while honoring your own boundaries?

____

____

____

____

Wrap Up

As you think about adopting a disposition of support, make sure that your own PF is at least 7 or higher. Be aware that you may need to take steps to fortify your mind before extending yourself to stressful circumstances even if your circumstances are much less overwhelming than that of your loved one. When you're ready, it may help to put yourself in their shoes to shift your perspective in a way that facilitates helping them. If you are feeling apprehensive about extending yourself to address their difficulty, consider what you would need to be open to receiving support from someone else. It's okay to pace yourself. You don't have to do everything at once. The first step is to be someone that your loved one knows they can count on at their time of greatest need.

CHAPTER 9

Step into a New Way of Living

When self-help influencers talk about "doing your work," they are typically referring to your intentional self-evaluation, the extraction of problematic beliefs and behaviors that no longer serve you, and rebuilding a healthier you. This work takes time because, while you can readily complete some of it, you're likely not fully ready to tackle other aspects. It's important to take stock of the work you've accomplished in the last eight chapters. If you began this book in a place of suffering, the skills you've learned have shown you a way of not only coping with low PF and mental health struggles, but also the blueprint for a more joyful life.

Remember in chapter 1 when you imagined yourself at the end of this book? You are closer to that vision now that you have learned and practiced a lot of different skills to minimize anxious thoughts and depressive feelings. You've set self-care goals and habits that will help fill an empty cup, reconnect with your authentic self, and make future challenges easier to hurdle. You may have to revisit some chapters again (and again!), but that is an understandable part of the journey to your best self.

Though racial stress certainly takes its toll, the practice of connecting with your African cultural roots will buffer the dehumanization that goes with living in the US and wherever Black people are in the numerical minority. And lastly, we've explored spiritual resources and your capacity to use them for increased resilience in daily life—resilience that comes easiest *when your PF is high.*

Congratulations on doing something different—for yourself, for your children, for your nieces and nephews, and for generations to come. Hopefully you've recognized that for some problems, there are no right or wrong answers; instead, you can respond in a way that protects and increases (rather than sabotages) your psychological fortitude. After working through this book, you have options. You can choose. You are now on a path to creating your own system of living in a way that is aligned with your higher PF.

Remembering Why You Started This Journey

Though this book is coming to an end, the process of navigating life is not. I wish it weren't true, but your journey is going to throw more at you than you would like and also at unexpected times. There will be more struggles, more disappointment, and more times your PF will dip below 5. The biggest takeaway that I want you to get from this book is that no matter what, you are going to be OK. With the strategies in this book, you have a new game plan to restore your mind and emerge from challenges feeling mentally intact and maybe even stronger overall. Just be sure to offer grace and a calm kindness to yourself until your skills kick in.

When these challenging moments come up, it'll be easy to revert to old habits. Old habits are on autopilot, so just be aware. They haven't served you long term, and they won't serve you moving forward. Those old habits are only temporary fixes. Continue to stay in contact with the exact reasons you picked this book up: your personal values.

In chapter 1, you explored your values. Your values will be your best roadmap as you integrate the skills you learned in this book into your life decisions. So, let's reintroduce our true selves. Remember our values are ours alone. They are our personally held beliefs about how we want to live our lives. Let's take some time to clarify them. You can do this exercise whenever you want to refresh or reassess your values. You can download a copy of it at http://www.newharbinger.com/50874.

What Are Your Values?

What does a well-lived life look like to you?

____

____

____

____

____

____

____

____

____

What kind of person do you wish to be known as?

Use these fill-ins to list some of your values.

I am/want to be ______

I am/want to be ______

I am/want to be ______

I am/want to be ______

I am/want to be ______

Looking at that list, what are a few things you can do to live out those values that you are not already doing or that you want to do more consistently?

Is there anything you can do today, tomorrow, or in the near future that could set you on a path to better actualizing one or more of your values?

____

____

____

____

____

____

Values Make Hard Decisions Easy

It is very possible that some of your values may change over time. That would not be surprising. The beauty of exploring and practicing your values is that, though they may change, their power to give a foundation to our lives remains unchanged. If you have ready access to the things you really care about, they freely guide your life. I, for instance, want to be someone who helps save lives and empowers others to do the same. My awareness and commitment to this value makes certain things—like writing this book, keeping up with the latest statistics, and engaging in suicide research—easy because those things conform to my ultimate vision of who I am.

Furthermore, the more you can be honest with yourself about what really matters, hard decisions are easier—career decisions, how you parent (or choose not to become a parent), who you partner with, you name it. These can be very hard and nuanced decisions. But sometimes simply viewing them through the lens of *Does this particular choice take me toward or away from that I truly care about?* makes the decision-making process less stressful.

Making Hard Decisions with Values

In this exercise, you are going to practice making value decisions using an example: meet Malaika. Malaika is a busy professional who doesn't have a lot of extra time but wants to be someone who cultivates her spiritual health and wellness above all else.

Malaika's values: *I want to be someone who devotes time and energy to a healthy spiritual practice.*

Opportunity: Malaika was invited by a friend to join a yoga class.

Malaika's automatic self-dialogue: *I don't know enough about yoga to go to a class. I will be nervous and look like a fool trying to do those moves.*

What would be most helpful for Malaika to do?

Is there an intention or positive thought Malaika could remind herself of to make her decision?

If Malaika wanted to go a step further, how might she consider living more aligned to her values?

Now it's your turn.

Is there a difficult or "heavy" opportunity or decision weighing on you? Write it down here:

Which of your values is at stake in this decision?

What thoughts, anxieties, or worries do you have about this decision?

If you were to decide in a way that is congruent with what you ultimately care about, what choice would you make? How would you ultimately feel about taking that path?

____

____

____

____

____

____

Accept That People Might Not Be on Board with Your Thriving

Don't be discouraged by naysayers or distracted by folks who take you away from your new direction. You can choose to engage them with the new understanding that you gain from this text, or you can conclude for yourself that they are fearful and not ready to do things differently. That does not make them wrong or combative. They're just not where you are. This is worth repeating to keep you from getting dragged into a useless argument: *They are not wrong or ignorant or angry or any of those negative labels. They are simply not where I am.* You can move forward with new approaches to living your life and taking care of your family without being distracted by those who are stuck in doing things the way that they have always been done.

Our community has a long history and a devoted relationship with stigma, denial, and shame when it comes to health and emotional health issues. Behind the proud belief that we are a strong people is a practiced habit of hiding our illnesses and struggles, explaining away the troubling behaviors of our loved ones, and suffering our secrets in silence. Stigma is an unbelievable force in our community that says you cannot get help. If you are real about it, stigma says there is no problem. I do think that we are seeing a decrease in the power of stigma, but the decrease is moving at a glacial pace.

For your journey to a high PF to be successful, you are going to have to accept that others will not support your journey. Lean on those boundary skills you worked on. Make your intentions with people clear and express how they can support you. Those not on board with supporting you can decline your boundary requests—and guess what, you just learned something very important about the kind of person they are.

Accept Help If People Want to Give It

If you are like me, you have to work at asking for help. I tell myself two things, especially when I am least inclined to ask for help:

1. I can struggle over something for days or ask someone else who can move it along in an hour or less.
2. I would want someone to ask me for help if they truly needed it and I could help. I would feel bad if they didn't ask. Instead, I can give someone an opportunity to help and maybe, just maybe, they will ask me when they need me!

One day, I would like for us to be able to talk about our psychological fortitude and how it is genuinely at 8 to 9 on most days and 5 on occasional days. We would acknowledge that there are days that are harder than others but that we know the tough days are temporary. If we ever feel that it is not temporary, we would feel comfortable reaching out to someone else rather than bingeing on chips and cookies.

Write down the names of three or more people who might help you. Then identify what they might be able to help with specifically.

1. ______________________________
2. ______________________________
3. ______________________________
4. ______________________________
5. ______________________________

Wrap Up

When you picked up this workbook, you were already on a path to a more meaningful life—a life in which you struggle less, have more energy, and feel clear-minded. Your spiritual self has been guiding you in this direction for some time. Even if you're not ready for all the change, you can notice the results of small steps that you build on for bigger results. You are on a path to your greatest and most authentic self. There will be detours and roadblocks. You may run out of gas or simply need to stop for rest. But you have an extensive set of tools to keep you going when you're ready. Because your path is personalized for you, it isn't going anywhere without you.

Conclusion

For too long, you have endured a life of emotional and psychological struggle. You came from a legacy of struggle wherein you learned how to bottle emotions and not "look like what you're going through." But now—now you are committed to maximizing your psychological fortitude and living your life tuned in to a higher frequency and tuning out negative external (and internal) chatter. You see yourself as the daring trailblazer in your life, letting go of how you have always done things to experiment with new possibilities.

You will encounter stressful situations and toxic people along the way, but you rebound faster from these encounters. Getting off track is part of the natural flow of life. You'll have heartbreak or illness followed by unexpected job opportunities and seasons of abundance. In the tough times, you'll use your new strategies until you are back on track, and you'll give yourself the same grace that you would give to others. You've learned to turn grace inward.

Remember to assess your psychological fortitude at regular intervals. If your rating is lower than you would like, recommit yourself to making adjustments, removing sources of aggravation, and tapping into your peace of mind. Revisit your most helpful worksheets and bookmark the ones that you may need for a season of life that you have not yet encountered. Remember to seek help when you need it. Avoid waiting until your PF has dipped so low that you find yourself on the verge of giving up hope that your circumstances can be better. You deserve long-lasting joy.

For now, celebrate! Honor each of your successes and every time you triumph over something that would have sabotaged your PF in the past. You're ready for change for you...and for the generations that will follow your trailblazing, psychologically fortified path.

Resources

There will be times when your PF is so low that expert—even emergency—resources are necessary. Below is a list of resources that can help you get the help you need.

Mental Health Directories with Black Practitioners

http://melaninandmentalhealth.com

http://blackmentalhealth.com

http://therapyforblackgirls.com

http://therapyforblackmen.org

http://blackfemaletherapists.com

http://inclusivetherapists.com

http://therapyincolor.org

http://cliniciansofcolor.org

http://innopsych.com

http://openpathcollective.org *(for low-cost/sliding-scale options)*

Community Organizations Prioritizing Black Wellness

African American Advocacy Center for Persons with Disabilities, https://blackdisabilitycenter.org

National Alliance on Mental Illness (NAMI) for Blacks, http://nami.org/Your-Journey/Identity-and-Cultural-Dimensions/Black-African-American

Reclaim the Block, https://www.reclaimtheblock.org

The Center for Black Health and Equity, https://www.centerforblackhealth.org

Ujima Community (The National Center on Violence Against Women in the Black Community), https://ujimacommunity.org

LGBTQIA2S+ Resources

Sayftee, http://www.sayftee.com

The Trevor Project Lifeline (24/7/365 connection to LGBTQIA+-related crisis support), 866-488-7386, http://thetrevorproject.org

LGBT National Hotline, 888-843-4564

National Queer and Trans Therapists of Color Network (NQTTCN), http://nqttcn.com

Society for Sexual, Affectional, Intersex, and Gender Expansive Identities (SAIGE), http://saigecounseling.org

FORGE (resources for trans+ survivors of violence and their loved ones), http://forge-forward.org

Suicide and Self-Harm Resources

Call or text 988 for the Suicide and Crisis Prevention Hotline (connection to a crisis counselor)

National Suicide Prevention Lifeline, 800-799-4889 (TTY), http://suicidepreventionlifeline.org

Disaster Distress Helpline (24/7/365 crisis counseling for emotional distress), 800-985-5990, text TALKWITHUS to 66746

Endnotes

Chapter 1

1 Ward, E. C., J. C. Wiltshire, M. A. Detry, and R. L. Brown. 2013. "African American Men and Women's Attitude Toward Mental Illness, Perceptions of Stigma, and Preferred Coping Behaviors." *Nursing Research* 62 (3): 185–194. http://doi.org/10.1097/NNR.0b013e31827bf533.

2 Boyers, J. 1999. *Coping Styles Questionnaire*. Kaiser-Permanente Medical Center and Health Styles, Santa Clara, CA.

Chapter 3

3 Pollack, M. H. 2005. "Comorbid Anxiety and Depression." *Journal of Clinical Psychiatry* 66: 22–29.

4 Newman, M. G., A. R. Zuellig, K. E. Kachin, M. J. Constantino, A. Przeworski, T. Erickson, and L. Cashman-McGrath. 2002. "Preliminary Reliability and Validity of the Generalized Anxiety Disorder Questionnaire-IV: A Revised Self-Report Diagnostic Measure of Generalized Anxiety Disorder." *Behavior Therapy* 33: 215–233. https://doi.org/10.1016/S0005-7894(02)80026-0.

5 Baker, F. M. 2001. "Diagnosing Depression in African Americans." *Community Mental Health Journal* 37: 31–38.

6 Breslau, J., K. N. Javaras, D. Blacker, J. M. Murphy, and S.-L. T. Normand. 2008. "Differential Item Functioning Between Ethnic Groups in the Epidemiological Assessment of Depression." *The Journal of Nervous and Mental Disease* 196 (4): 297–306.

7 Bor, J., A. S. Venkataramani, D. R. Williams, and A. C. Tsai. 2018. "Police Killings and Their Spillover Effects on the Mental Health of Black Americans: A Population-Based, Quasi-Experimental Study." *The Lancet* 392 (10144): 302–310.

8 Bor, "Police Killings and Their Spillover Effects on the Mental Health of Black Americans."

9 Tynes, B. M., H. A. Willis, A. M. Stewart, and M. W. Hamilton. 2019. "Race-Related Traumatic Events Online and Mental Health Among Adolescents of Color." *Journal of Adolescent Health* 65 (3): 371–377.

Chapter 4

10 Prochaska, J. O., and J. C. Norcross. 2001. "Stages of Change." *Psychotherapy: Theory, Research, Practice, Training* 38 (4): 443–448. https://doi.org/10.1037/0033-3204.38.4.443.

11 Yeager, D. S., and C. S. Dweck. 2020. "What Can Be Learned from Growth Mindset Controversies?" *American Psychologist* 75 (9): 1269–1284.

Chapter 5

12 Bailey, Z. D., N. Krieger, M. Agénor, J. Graves, N. Linos, and M. T. Bassett. 2015. "Structural Racism and Health Inequities in the USA: Evidence and Interventions." *The Lancet* 389, no. 10077: 1453–1463.

13 Paradies, Y., J. Ben, N. Denson, A. Elias, N. Priest, A. Pieterse, A. Gupta, M. Kelaher, and G. Gee. 2015. "Racism as a Determinant of Health: A Systematic Review and Meta-Analysis." *PLoS One* 10: e0138511.

14 Schulz, A. J., C. C. Gravlee, D. R. Williams, B. A. Israel, G. Mentz, and Z. Rowe. 2006. "Discrimination, Symptoms of Depression, and Self-Rated Health Among African American Women in Detroit: Results from a Longitudinal Analysis." *American Journal of Public Health* 96 (7): 1265–1270.

15 Lewis, T. T., S. A. Everson-Rose, L. H. Powell, K. A. Matthews, C. Brown, K. Karavolos, K. Sutton-Tyrrell, E. Jacobs, and D. Wesley. 2006. "Chronic Exposure to Everyday Discrimination and Coronary Artery Calcification in African-American Women: The SWAN Heart Study." *Psychosomatic Medicine* 68 (3): 362–368.

16 Sue, D. W., C. M. Capodilupo, G. C. Torino, J. M. Bucceri, A. M. B. Holder, K. L. Nadal, et al. 2007. "Racial Microaggressions in Everyday Life: Implications for Clinical Practice." American Psychologist 62(4): 271–286.

17 Singh, A. A. 2019. *The Racial Healing Handbook: Practical Activities to Help You Challenge Privilege, Confront Systemic Racism, and Engage in Collective Healing.* Oakland, CA: New Harbinger Publications.

18 Walker, R. L., L. R. Wingate, E. M. Obasi, and T. E. Joiner, Jr. 2008. "An Empirical Investigation of Acculturative Stress and Ethnic Identity as Moderators for Depression and Suicidal Ideation in College Students." *Cultural Diversity and Ethnic Minority Psychology* 14 (1): 75–82.

Chapter 6

19 King James Version Bible, 1987, Ex. 14:14.

20 Mattis, J. S. 2000. "African American Women's Definitions of Spirituality and Religiosity." *Journal of Black Psychology* 26 (1): 118.

21 King James Version Bible, 1987, Romans 12:2.

22 King James Version Bible, 1987, James 2:17.

23 Coelho, P. 2014. *The Alchemist*. New York: HarperOne, 214.

24 King James Version Bible, 1987, Prov.3:5.

Rheeda Walker, PhD, is an award-winning professor of psychology at the University of Houston, and author of the self-help phenomenon, *The Unapologetic Guide to Black Mental Health*. She is a behavioral science researcher, licensed clinical psychologist, and has published more than sixty scientific papers on African American adult mental health from a culturally meaningful perspective, suicide risk, and psychological resilience. Walker is a fellow in the American Psychological Association, the leading scientific and professional organization of psychologists in the US.

Walker's expertise has been cited in countless media outlets, including *The Washington Post*, NPR, *Los Angeles Times, Houston Chronicle*, and *Ebony* magazine. She has been a guest expert psychologist on *Good Morning America, The Breakfast Club*, and *Red Table Talk*. She has trained and mentored clinical psychology doctoral students toward independent clinical and research careers since 2003, and is well known for engaging keynotes and workshops that address emotional wellness and culturally informed interventions. Visit her online at www.drrheedawalker.com.

Foreword writer **Angela Neal-Barnett, PhD**, is a national award-winning psychologist, professor, and leading expert on anxiety disorders among Black Americans. She directs the Program for Research on Anxiety Disorders among African Americans (PRADAA) at Kent State University. Neal-Barnett's current work focuses on the role of racism and trauma in Black infant mortality and maternal morbidity, as well as culturally competent anxiety intervention.